THE Keyboard Handbook

Steve Lodder and
Janette Mason

The Keyboard Handbook
Steve Lodder and Janette Mason

A BACKBEAT BOOK
First edition 2012
Published by Backbeat Books
An Imprint of Hal Leonard Corporation
7777 West Bluemound Road,
Milwaukee, WI 53213
www.backbeatbooks.com

Devised and produced for Backbeat Books by
Outline Press Ltd
2A Union Court, 20-22 Union Road,
London SW4 6JP, England
www.jawbonepress.com

ISBN: 978-1-61713-104-2

A catalogue record for this book is available from the British Library.

DESIGN: Paul Cooper Design
EDITOR: Tom Seabrook

Printed by Everbest Printing Co. Ltd, China

12 13 14 15 16 5 4 3 2 1

CONTENTS

INTRODUCTION

Welcome to *The Keyboard Handbook*. In the course of this book, most 20th and 21st-century popular musical styles will be covered, from gospel to glam-rock. Because some styles are more complex than others, some units will be easier to master than others, but we have attempted to build in progressive difficulty through the examples.

This book includes a basic guide to reading music. It shows you the names of the notes on the stave and the basic rhythmic divisions. If you feel under-equipped, look no further than Dave Stewart's *The Musician's Guide To Reading And Writing Music*, where help is at hand.

Before we start, a few words about posture. As careers develop, artists carve out their own way of sitting at the keyboard. For instance, Keith Emerson, the prog-rock keyboardist extraordinaire, is often to be found standing at a Hammond, or a bank of synths, or even both simultaneously. Meanwhile Keith Jarrett, the equally famous jazz pianist, can often be found contorting himself above the keyboard and even below it.

These are not good examples to follow. Any authority will tell you that the line from your forearm and hand to the knuckles should be approximately straight. Bending at the wrist, as practiced by the two Keiths, should be avoided at all costs. Of course, nobody plays like that all the time, but it's still a worrying physical attitude.

So what's the ideal keyboard-playing posture? Apart from the line through the wrist to knuckle, other points are: sitting on a stool wide enough to support a degree of lateral movement for high and low notes;

feet near the pedals but heels resting on the ground; shoulders and neck relaxed, free of tension. This last is probably the most important. Keyboard playing is a physical exercise and requires the body to return to a state of relaxation once the act of playing a note (or several thousand) has been performed. You can't practice for hours at a time while tense, and sooner or later you're going to want to play for hours at a time. Paying a certain amount of attention to the realm of the physical can help to avoid problems later on.

Some keyboards are more taxing than others. A light, unweighted synth action, as implemented on the majority of home and professional keyboards, is easier to tame than an 88-note weighted piano action. Even so, you will need to do a certain amount of physical as well as musical practice to whip those digits into shape. As for which type of keyboard you should choose to own and practice on, that's a question with too many variables to answer here; suffice to say that the piano has served as a good training instrument for years, while keyboard students can have problems switching to piano. On a listening level, the piano also has many more degrees of audio subtlety and touch variation, but it obviously lacks the changes of costume available to a synth player. In the end, just play, and if you're relaxed, your technique will adapt itself to the instrument.

Unit One will lean towards the making of chords, as that's what keyboard players do best. Armed with those basic chords and inversions, you could be accompanying a singer—or playing with other musicians—in no time at all.

LEARNING THE KEYBOARD

The first task for the beginner is to learn to find your way around the keyboard. Below is a sample of how it looks and an explanation of how to find your way around it. Practice finding every A on your keyboard, then every B, every C, and so on. Make a special note of the C right in the middle of the keyboard. This is "Middle C."

PRACTICING READING

You'll have noticed that notes to the right are progressively higher in pitch, while notes to the left get progressively lower. This is reflected in music notation. Notes are indicated by their vertical position on a set of five horizontal lines known as the "stave" or "staff" (always pronounced "stave"). They can appear on the lines or in the spaces between them. In keyboard music we normally have two staves running parallel: one for the right hand and one for the left. Each has a different sign at the start of the line of music, called a "clef." This is important, as the letter-names come in different places on the staff depending on whether they are for right hand (with treble clef) or left hand (bass clef).

Note that reading just the notes on spaces, or just the notes on lines, in ascending order, gives a pattern of letter names that we can memorize; we can either read the pattern as a word, or make each letter the beginning of a word in a phrase (see below).

The Keyboard

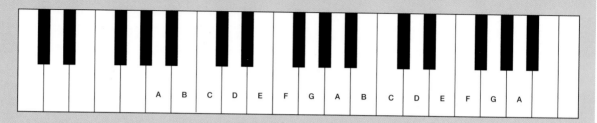

Notice how black keys alternate with white keys, except where two white keys sit next to each other with no black key between them. This creates larger gaps between some of the black keys, which fall into a nice alternating pattern of groups of two and three. We use this pattern to locate the different notes or pitches. Note how we use the first seven letters of the alphabet to refer just to the white notes. (We'll learn the black notes later.) You can see that when we come back to the same place in the pattern we reach the same letter-name again; we call this distance between two notes with the same place in the pattern and the same letter-name an "octave." The piano has seven octaves plus four more keys in its 88-note keyboard. Many keyboards have 61 keys, spanning five octaves.

Treble Clef (Right Hand)

Bass Clef (Left Hand)

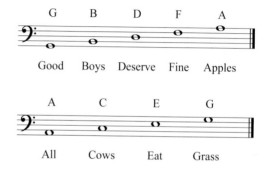

The diagram below shows how the two clefs fit together. Middle C comes above the bass clef and below the treble clef, with a small line through it. This line is called a "leger line," and represents an extra horizontal line that runs between the right and left-hand staves but which is only shown when it is needed for particular notes.

Sometimes the notes need to continue beyond the staves, and so extra leger lines are added to accommodate them, as shown right (Leger lines 1). This can simply be because the notes are too high or low to be shown on the clefs.

But leger lines are also used when the left hand plays above Middle C or the right plays below (Leger lines 2).

Treble And Bass Clef Together

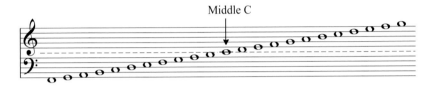

Leger Lines 1

Leger Lines 2

PRACTICING COUNTING

We normally control rhythm in music by relating notes of varying durations to a regular underlying pulse. This pulse falls into regular cycles of beats, which we call the "meter" of the music. When learning music, it often helps to count out these beats silently, in our head (or even aloud), while we are playing, to make sure that our timing is accurate. Later we learn to feel how the rhythm relates to the meter.

This is reflected in the way the music is written: it has regular divisions, called "measures" or "bars," separated by vertical lines called "barlines." Each bar corresponds to a metrical cycle. A double barline indicates the end of a piece or section of a piece. Two dots before a double barline, whether at the end of

the piece or before the end, indicate that you should return to the start and repeat either that section or the whole piece. A double bar with two dots after it indicates that you should start your repeat from there, not from the start of the piece.

Rhythms are expressed as different time-values corresponding to successive halvings of the longest commonly used time-value, which is known as the whole-note in America and northern Europe and the semibreve in Britain and some other countries. In the American system, the names for the smaller time-values simply reflect those successive halvings: whole-note, half-note, quarter-note, etc. In the British system, different names are used for each time-value, derived from French and Latin.

Time-Value Divisions

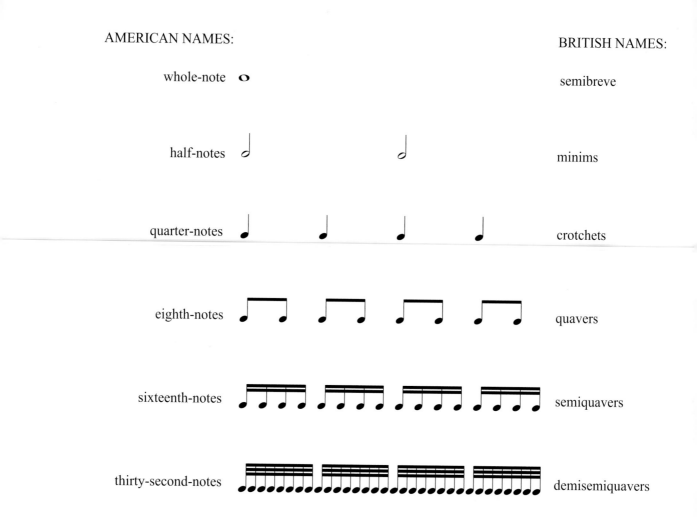

AMERICAN NAMES:		BRITISH NAMES:
whole-note		semibreve
half-notes		minims
quarter-notes		crotchets
eighth-notes		quavers
sixteenth-notes		semiquavers
thirty-second-notes		demisemiquavers

For every note, there is an equivalent "rest," indicating a period of silence of exactly the same duration. (A rest lasting for a whole bar is always shown with the sign for a whole-note rest, even when the bar itself is longer or shorter.)

In practice, it's often easier to think of time-values as divisions or multiples of whatever time-value represents the actual pulse of the music. This time-value, along with the number of beats per bar, is indicated at the start by the "time signature": two numbers that look and work rather like a fraction.

The lower number states the time-value corresponding to one unit of the pulse, as a division of the longest time-value, as in the diagram on the previous page. The upper number shows how many of these fit into one bar. Here are some common time signatures. Note the alternative names and signs for some of them.

To indicate note durations that are not available using the basic time-values, you have to join notes together, using a curved line called a "tie." For instance, to indicate a duration of three quarter-notes, you can tie a half-note to a quarter-note. This rhythmic pattern, in which a note is extended by half its length, is very common. Another way of indicating it is to use a dot: placing a dot after any time-value adds half as much again to the value of the note. Placing a dot after a rest also adds half as much again to its length.

Rests

NOTE:	REST:

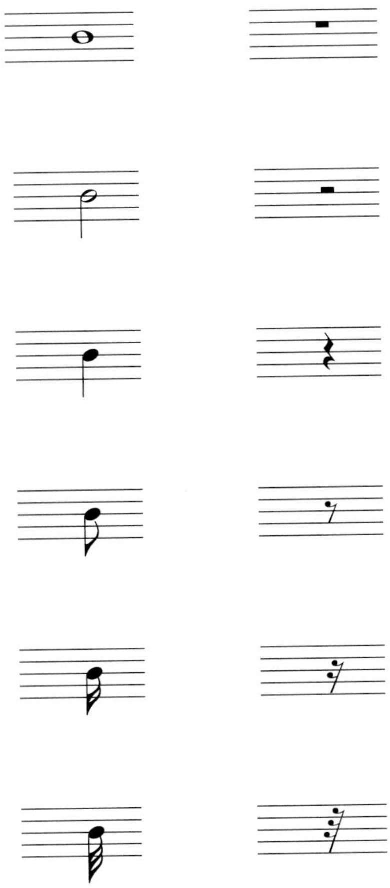

Time Signatures

SIMPLE DUPLE TIME:

2 eighth-note beats per bar

$\frac{2}{8}$

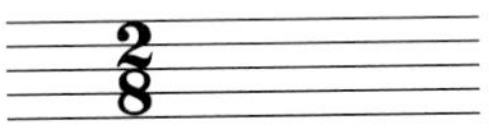

2 quarter-note beats per bar

$\frac{2}{4}$

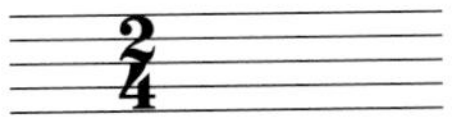

2 half-note beats per bar   *alla breve*

$\frac{2}{2}$ **or**   ¢

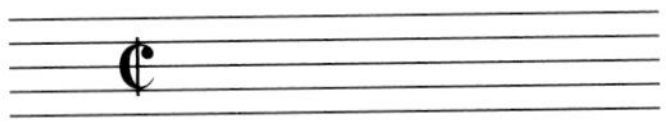

SIMPLE TRIPLE TIME:

3 eighth-note beats per bar

$\frac{3}{8}$

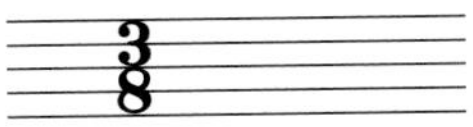

3 quarter-note beats per bar

$\frac{3}{4}$

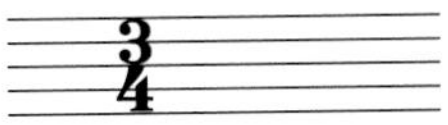

SIMPLE QUADRUPLE TIME:

4 quarter-note beats per bar

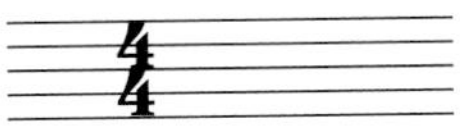

$\frac{4}{4}$

'common time'

or   C

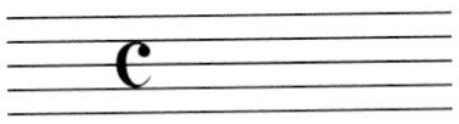

CLAPPING

Let's practice clapping different rhythms, counting the beats of the bar aloud at the same time, so we can hear how the rhythms relate to them. With each new bar we start over again, counting from "one." We can also count divisions within a beat if necessary: where a beat is divided in two we count "one-and two-and" etc. Where a beat is divided into four we count "one-e-and-a." Those divisions within a beat can be grouped in different ways, as this clapping exercise demonstrates. Clap on the syllable written above the note. Notice the curved line in the fourth line, connecting the last note of the second bar to the first note of the next: this is a tie. It means that instead of playing or clapping the second note you hold the first note on for the combined value of both.

When reading the music in this book it is a good idea to clap the rhythms first to work them out. You can use the CD tracks to check that you have it right.

Clapping Different Rhythms

THE BLACK NOTES

Take a look at the diagram, which shows that each of the five different black notes can have two possible names. This is because we think of black notes as alterations of neighboring white notes; we treat each one as an alteration of the white note either to the left (just below) or to the right (just above). In the former case it is as if we were slightly raising the pitch of the white note, so we call it a "sharp." In the latter case it is as if we were slightly lowering it, so we call it a "flat."

In written music we place sharp and flat signs just in front of the notehead, on the same line or space. A "natural" sign cancels a sharp or flat, meaning that you just play the normal white note.

We can write the signs for sharps, flats, and naturals in front of individual notes, in which case they are known as "accidentals," and affect that particular note (in that particular octave only) for the remainder of the bar, unless cancelled by another sign. However, most music sticks to one scale—which we call its key—for a lot of the time.

Each key has its own pattern of sharps or flats, so it is simpler to show these at the beginning of each line of music. We call this a "key signature." This means you must remember to apply these alterations automatically to any note in the music with the corresponding letter-name (in any octave).

It's important to remember, however, that these signs can still be overridden by accidentals in the music, which will affect a particular note right up to the end of the bar in which the accidental appears.

Black Notes

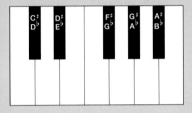

Sharp, Flat, And Natural Signs

sharp   flat   natural

Sharps, Flats, And Naturals In Music

sharp   natural   flat   natural

THE FIRST SCALE

You'll recognize the first scale, because every music theory book known to man begins with it, and we're not about to be any different.

You guessed it: it's the C major scale. But if you were Greek and living about 2,500 years back, you might have called it the Ionian mode. What makes it a major scale is the particular pattern of steps you get when you play just the white notes. Some of the white notes have black notes between them (making them a whole step apart), while some don't (making them a half-step or semitone apart).

The pattern for a major scale is whole step / whole step /

half-step / whole step / whole step / whole step / half-step (tone / tone / semitone / tone / tone / tone / semitone).

You can start a major scale on any note, but in order to produce the correct pattern of whole and half-steps you will have to use sharps and flats. These are shown in the key signature for each key. On the left are the key signatures for the most common major keys.

The small numbers written above and below the notes in the scale are instructions as to fingering. Each hand is numbered outwards from the thumb (1), through the index (2), middle (3), and ring (4) fingers to the little finger or "pinkie" (5).

Example 1.1, C Major Scale

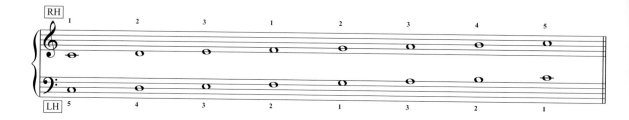

Key Signatures

Sharp keys

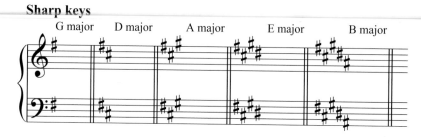

Flat keys

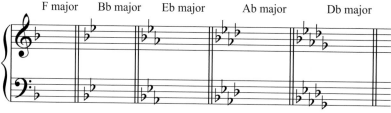

The next scale was once known as the Aeolian mode, but in the 21st century we call it the A natural minor scale or alternatively the minor melodic descending. (There are other types of minor scale that require accidentals.) Because C major and A natural minor share the same notes, but start on a different step or "degree" of the scale, A minor is said to be the "relative minor" of C major. The relative minor of a major scale is always three half-steps (semitones) lower.

Many a player has run screaming from the building at the mere mention of scales, but it's important to see them as your friendly adviser; not a dry, dusty, theoretical enemy but a companion, here to guide you around the keyboard and organize your musical invention.

The most important aspect of learning scales is to play the ascending right hand E–F or descending left hand A–G without any lumps. This entails passing the thumb under smoothly: it's natural for the elbow to want to kick out when the thumb passes under the third finger. Practice C up to F in your right hand and C down to G in your left hand until the movement feels natural or you feel like screaming.

Either way, play both major and minor scales slowly, watching out for hand/finger positions and any major distortions.

Example 1.2, A Natural Minor Scale

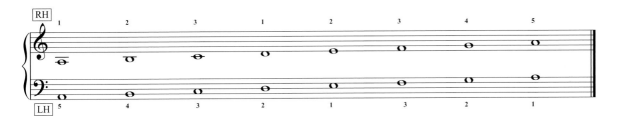

A Natural Minor On The Keyboard

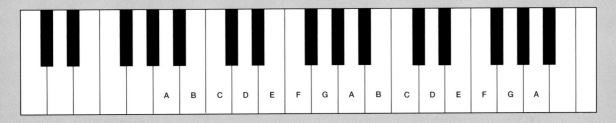

Look at the keyboard diagram above and you will see that the pattern of steps for the A natural minor scale looks like this: whole step / half-step / whole step / whole step / half-step / whole step / whole step (tone / semitone / tone / tone / semitone / tone / tone). Again, you can build a natural minor scale on any note, using the same pattern of steps and half-steps, but you will need to use sharps or flats to make it work. A minor scale has the same key signature as its relative major, ie, the major scale that starts three half-steps (semitones) higher.

These two examples are tunes to get you up and running. Example 1.3a is in the key of C major, bright and jaunty as only C major can be, while Example 1.3b is based firmly in the minor, with a touch of melancholy.

Example 1.3a uses three basic right-hand positions: in the first bar the fingers cover C–G, in bars two and three they cover G–D, and in bar four the hand moves to D–A. The quarter-note rest in bar two leaves time for the hand to move, but don't hang about; as soon as the previous G is gone, move up. For bar four the fourth finger has to come over the thumb; again, watch for smoothness.

Clap the rhythms before you start. The left-hand part is not too challenging, although the rhythm will have to be kept steady. Practice the left hand first to get the pattern embedded; then you can consign it to the darker recesses and concentrate on the right hand.

In Example 1.3b the right hand gets around a bit, so follow the fingering for the best route. While we're on the subject, of course everybody has their favorite fingerings, some more convoluted than others. The suggested fingerings throughout this book are the result of years of experience and gathered wisdom on behalf of the composers, but you may decide you want to forge your own path. Just don't say we didn't warn you.

Example 1.3a, Major Tune

Example 1.3b, Minor Tune

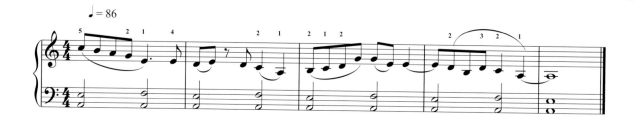

BUILDING CHORDS

Let's take another look at that C major scale in order to build up some chords. C is the root note, which is also the first degree of the scale, so we'll call it 1. The other notes shown in boxes are the third and fifth degrees of the scale. When all three are played together, they form a major "triad."

The major triad is built out of two intervals, a major third (four half-steps/semitones) between C and E, and a minor third (three half-steps/semitones) between E and G. The fingering is handily the same as the description of the scale degrees, so curve your 1, 3, and 5 fingers around the chord and see how it feels. Now do it again. Now take your hand away and find the notes from scratch. Now do it again until it's automatic.

Next, do the same with the left hand and get to know the feel of a C major chord under the hand. Same fingers, other way up. If you want to play both hands together we're not about to stop you.

You can also build major triads on other roots. Take F for instance; the same pattern of half-steps/semitones takes us up to A for the third and C for the fifth. This is included here—with the notes of the triad played one at a time, rather than together—as a snippet bearing some resemblance to an Aaron Copland tune; indeed these notes appear just after the start of "Fanfare For The Common Man." Keith Emerson did a version with the group ELP. The "horseshoes" over the G and the final C are pause marks, so that's what you do.

Example 1.4, Major Scale And Triad

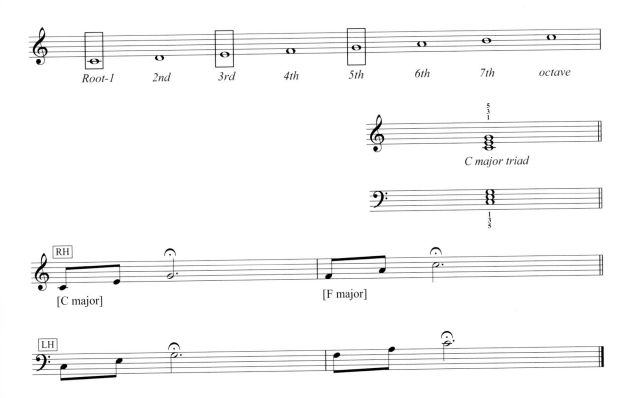

COMPOUND TIME

The example is in 12/8, an example of what is called "compound time," which means that each of the four basic beats in the measure is divided into three.

The piece uses "broken" or spread major triads, where the notes are played one at a time, firstly in the right hand then right hand and left hand together. They're all in 1–3–5 position, which is why the leaps are sometimes slightly awkward between hand positions.

Finger the 1–3–5 chord with a second finger instead of a third when it seems natural, to help with these changes of position. Try to keep the wrist and top of the hand quite stable, so that the action comes from the fingers, rather than rocking the whole hand side-to-side.

There are a few chords here. Along with C, F, and G we've sneaked in D, B-flat, and even E-flat to expand your chordal knowledge.

Example 1.5, "Broken Triads"

MINOR CHORDS

In the same way as you extract a 1–3–5 chord from the major scale, you can take one from the minor scale. Example 1.6a is the A natural minor scale with the 1–3–5 notes shown in boxes. Play the scale, then the chord, in both hands.

You can transform a major chord into a minor by lowering or flattening the third. You can turn a minor chord into a major by raising/sharpening the third. But first, let's look at all the semitones of the octave, as outlined in Example 1.6b. When you play all the notes, black as well as white, it's known as the "chromatic" scale.

You will notice that the black notes can have two names: if you're in a sharp key the semitone above C will be called C-sharp, and if you're in a flat key it will be called D-flat. The same applies to the other black notes.

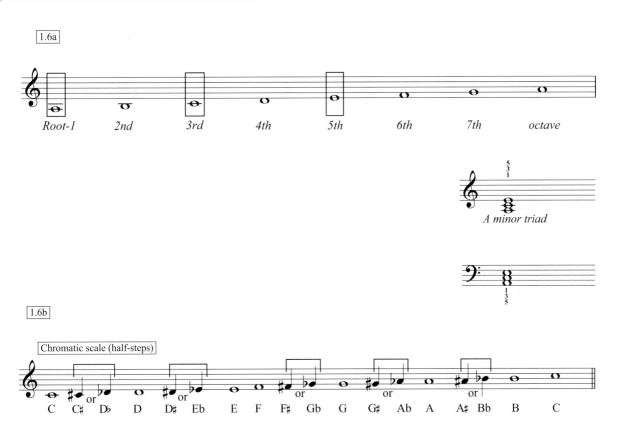

Check the fingering for the chromatic scale (left), and now we're ready to turn a C major chord into a minor chord.

Example 1.6c shows a C minor chord; the third has been flattened, turning it into an E-flat. Why not a D-sharp? Because every scale has to consist of seven different note-names in order. The second note in a C scale must be a D of some sort, whether natural, sharpened, or flattened. The third note must be

an E of some sort and so on up to the seventh, which must be a B of some sort. In the C minor chord, we are flattening the third; the third must be some sort of E, so the flattened third is E-flat.

One more nugget; the intervals in the minor triad are opposite to those in the major. It's three half-steps (or semitones) up to a minor third, then four half-steps—the equivalent of a major third—to the fifth.

1.6c

C minor triad

C minor triad

There's no reason why the minor triads shouldn't have a piece for themselves, so here one is. Both hands get to see a piece of the action, the right hand initially playing the chords while the left hand steps through in eighth-notes. Clap out the rhythms first.

Notice that the root of the chord is omitted in the right hand occasionally; that's because it's been stolen by the left hand, so there's either no space for it or no point in doubling it.

As with keys, take note of the relative majors of all the minor chords in this piece; for instance the B minor is relative to D major. Just take the minor root up a minor third (three half-steps) to get to the relative major.

Example 1.7, "Minor Triumph"

CHORD INVERSIONS

One of the problems with playing chords in their 1-3-5 or "root" position is that it can sound pretty basic. Also, it's awkward to move the hand around, as we saw in Example 1.5. Time to call for chord inversions, the answer to all your chordal problems.

In a first inversion C major, the C moves up an octave, leaving E on the bottom and G in the middle.

In a second inversion C major, the E also moves up an octave, leaving the G at the bottom and the C in the middle.

This is what the inversions look like in notation. The numbers to the right of the inversion name tell you the order of the intervals, counting from the bottom. 351, for instance, means that the third is at the bottom followed by the fifth and the root. Fingering is in small numbers above the chord.

Example 1.8b is the same process using a minor chord.

Practice both major and minor with both hands, with the left hand starting an octave lower than the right hand.

Example 1.8c is a real life use of a first inversion chord that might just ring a bell.

Example 1.8, Inversions

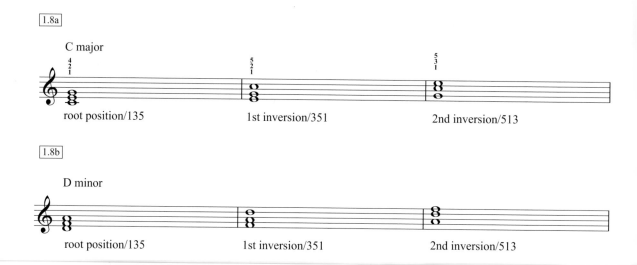

INVERSION PIECE

A bit of an inversion and rhythm workout, this one. You can see from bars one and two the immediate usefulness of using the first inversion on the C and the second on the B-flat. How satisfying to send the outer lines in contrary motion; that is, top line up and bottom line down. All over the place, chord changes are smoothed by the fact that the top line has become exceedingly lazy, moving vertically as little as possible.

Meanwhile, the "syncopation" of the right hand at the beginning—emphasizing the offbeats rather than the main beats—provides exercise for idle fingers. The roles of the two hands reverse as the piece progresses.

Example 1.9, "Quite Contrary"

SEVENTH CHORDS

Example 1.10a introduces seventh chords. The first chord is a C major triad with a B at the top, the B being the seventh note of the C major scale. The whole chord is called a "major seventh" chord. (The seventh is shown here as a black note.) In sheet music the symbol for the chord is Cmaj7.

In the next chord, the B has been flattened by a half-step (or a semitone) to become a B-flat, so instead of being a major seventh chord, it becomes what is called a "dominant seventh" chord. Often the dominant bit is left out and it is just called a seventh chord. The symbol for the C dominant seventh chord is C7.

So, just to clarify, in a major seventh the top note (in root position) is a half-step or semitone away from the octave of the root. In a (dominant) seventh chord in similar position the seventh is a whole step (or tone) away from the octave of the root.

There's a difference in function too; the major seventh chord seems happy with life where it is, while the seventh chord is pulling in a gravitational way to the major chord a fifth (five degrees of the scale) below. In other words, add a seventh to a G chord and it immediately wants to be followed by a C chord. Example 1.10b gives a few seventh and major seventh chord examples, then a couple of seventh chords followed by their "home" chords, the chords they are pulled toward.

Example 1.10, Major And Dominant Sevenths

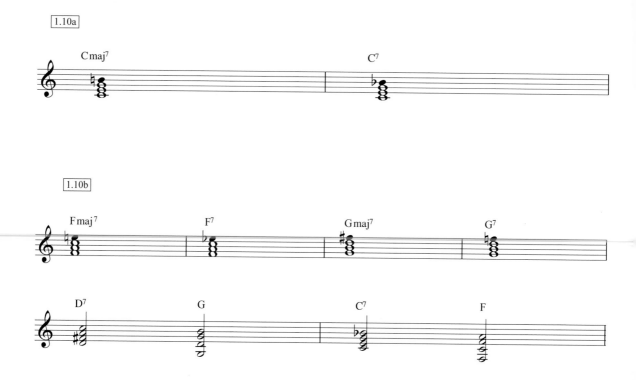

THE CIRCLE OF FIFTHS

This chart, called the Circle Of Fifths, shows the key signatures of all the major keys in order: clockwise they get sharper (adding a sharp each time); counter-clockwise they get flatter (adding a flat each time).

If you add a seventh to a C chord, making it a C7, feel how it wants to resolve on to an F, which is one step counter-clockwise around the wheel. Add a seventh to the F, making it an F7, and it will want to navigate to the B-flat, and so on all the way around the wheel. The seventh chord pulls around the wheel counterclockwise, adding flats as it goes.

Contrast that feeling of being dragged down with the effect of moving clockwise around the wheel; starting on C, just play triads, with your key becoming sharper as you go around. You can feel how things are getting brighter and better and warmer all the time.

The Circle Of Fifths should reside in every musician's head. It's a very good navigational aid through the seas of tonality.

Circle Of Fifths

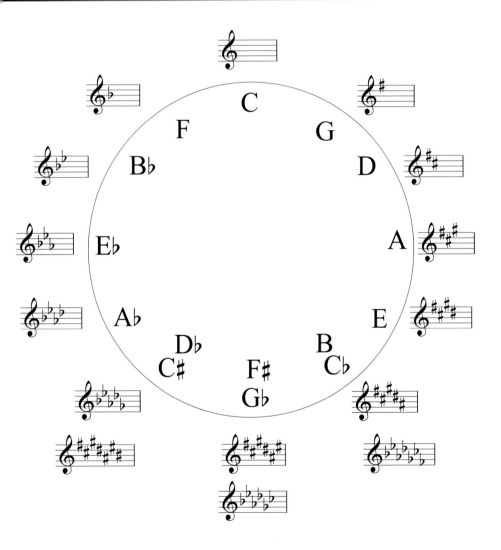

Example 1.11 is a typical example of a rocking (as in cradle, not rock'n'roll) right-hand pattern, typical of slower tunes. Major sevenths and sevenths are used. Notice that the seventh chord doesn't have to resolve to the chord a fifth below, it just wants

to. Bars five to nine feature a sneak preview of the next topic, seventh chord inversions, and a melody in the right hand—a fairly rare event so far.

Example 1.11, "Slow Sevenths"

INVERTED SEVENTHS

As promised, you can apply inversions to seventh or major seventh chords in exactly the same way as with major/minor triads. In the case of C major seventh (Cmaj7) in Example 1.12, take the bottom note, the root, and move it up an octave as before, then take the E and do the same with that, and so on. The major seventh, being a four-note chord, gives you a root position and three inversions. The same goes for the dominant seventh chord (C7), which is shown in a left-hand version.

The chart also includes two minor seventh chords. These are a minor triad with the seventh note of the natural minor scale added. They can also be inverted. Here you see inversions of the D minor seventh (Dm7) in the right hand and the A minor seventh (Am7) in the left hand. Pay particular attention to the left hand, particularly in the lower-mid register, as later on it's going to be playing a lot of this sort of chord.

Even though this is an exercise, it's probably worth playing this page in time, as the pressure of getting to the next chord on the next half-note will speed the learning process.

Example 1.12, Inverted Sevenths

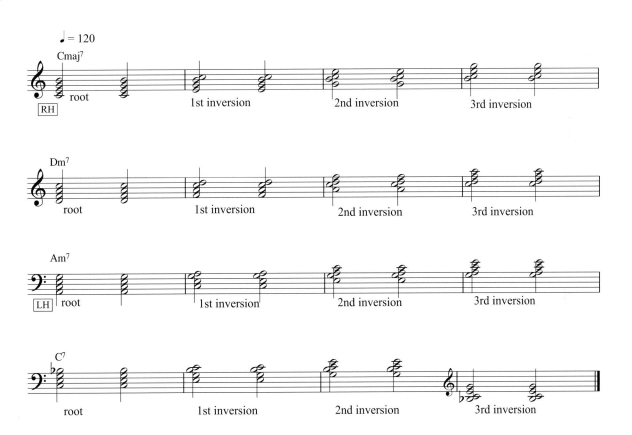

Having mastered all those inversions, try this piece. It has a church feel to it that would suit an organ sound, be it pipe or tonewheel. The melody at the top of the right-hand chords can now be free to plot its own destiny as the harmony beneath is inverted to follow the melody's dictates. Take it fairly slowly as there are a few notes in there to sort out.

If you have a Hammond organ sound on your keyboard, try turning on the Leslie revolving speaker effect. Fire it up in bar five or six and wind it down again in bar ten to wring every ounce of emotion from bars seven and eight.

Fingering can be quite personal in this example. It's not worth trying to keep the melody smooth in the right hand: phrase and finger with a gap in between each chord. If you keep the bass smooth for the first eight bars, it will help to hold things together.

Example 1.13, "Organ Donor"

ARPEGGIATION

You might have seen a function on a synth called an arpeggiator, which is a way of animating static chords in all sorts of wonderful ways. Believe it or not, humans are capable of this function too—and in even more unpredictable ways.

Not that Example 1.14a is *that* unpredictable. Far from it. To start with it takes the C major chord and singles out each note of each inversion. This is called a broken chord.

Example 1.14b is a slightly different pattern. Instead of backtracking every now and then, the arpeggio goes direct to destination in one journey. This relies on having good thumb-under technique, so it's important to play the broken chords in

other keys: G, F, Am, Dm, Em. This will give you enough mobility to play the arpeggios in the same keys.

Example 1.14c is back to broken chords, this time a Dm7 that obviously has one more note present than the basic chord. It's easier to negotiate physically than the arpeggio, and good to get under one's belt.

Here's a fancy trick: if you have an arpeggiator, play the C7 arpeggio yourself then switch on the machine and hold down a C7 chord. If you select the right pattern (such as two octaves up and down) it should mimic what you played. Then the ghastly truth: it's better at it than you are, but it doesn't *feel* it the same way.

Example 1.14, Arpeggios

Speaking of feel—which we were—Example 1.15 is a four-chord trick using fairly straight and unchallenging voicings after the gut-busting contortions of the previous page. The feel is South African, and thumb piano/mbira/kalimba would be a good choice of sound. Natural rhythmic interplay between the two hands is vital; the piece should flow like the Zambezi over Victoria Falls.

It could equally be written in 12/8, four groups of three eighth-notes, but 4/4 makes for easier reading at this stage. Note the repeat signs that tell you to play the first four bars twice and then to play bars five to eight twice.

The main thing is to have fun with it. Repeat each section and see whether you prefer the E minor in bar three or the A minor in bar six.

Notice how in the second group of four bars the seventh chords lead to the chord a fifth below.

Example 1.15, "Go With The Flow"

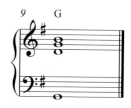

CHORD SYMBOLS

All the way along we have used chord symbols alongside the written notes to indicate the harmony. Example 1.16 shows what happens when you take away the notes and just leave the chord symbols. With no indication of feel, the choice is yours. With no indication of inversions, the way you get from one chord to the next is also yours.

Here are the chords and symbols used so far:
- a major chord is C.
- a minor chord is Cm.
- a major seventh chord is Cmaj7.
- a dominant seventh chord is C7.
- a minor seventh chord is Cm7.

Try the chord sequence below in the same South African feel. It's identical in harmony even though the key has been changed. Then try it in pop ballad style with block chords in the right hand and octave roots in the left hand.

Another way of looking at chord symbols is to describe them in relation to the tonal center of a piece. The key signature of Example 1.16 has one flat, which tells us that it is almost certainly in the key of F or its relative minor, D minor. The presence of the F chord in the first bar and the major feel of the piece all point to the tonal center, the key of the song, being F major. Using a chord chart gives you the freedom to choose your own inversions and make your own decisions about how to get from one chord to another.

Example 1.16, Chord Charts

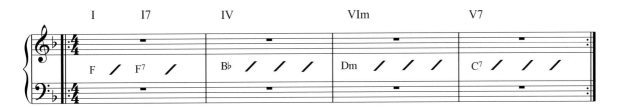

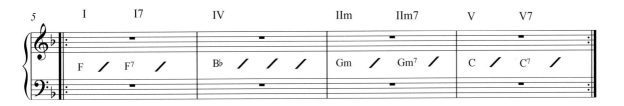

The Roman numerals you see written above each chord here let you describe a chord sequence in terms of each chord's relationship with the tonal center. In the key of F, the F chord is called chord I. The other chords in the key take their numbers from the degrees of the F scale; in this case the B-flat is a IV chord, being built on the fourth step of the scale, and the C a V chord. Add an 'm' to indicate a minor and a '7' to indicate a seventh and a Gm7 becomes IIm7.

This system is useful because it allows you to learn the relationships between chords, whatever key you are in. For instance, in G your IV chord would be C and your V would be D. In D, your IV chord would be G and your V chord would be A. And so on. This comes in very handy on a gig where you suddenly need to change the key of a song to suit a singer or instrumentalist. As long as your chart shows you the relationships between the chords, you should be able to find your way around.

We've all heard of the blues. But what does the term mean, and how widely has the blues influenced music throughout the 20th century and beyond?

The blues emerged in the United States in the early 1900s as a vocal and instrumental form of music, based on work songs and spirituals, that incorporated simple repetitive figures and introduced "blue notes" to European harmony.

Much of this early music is undocumented. However, thanks to the advent of the gramophone and the record industry's realization that the music had commercial value, we can still hear the great blues pianists of the day: Jelly Roll Morton, Meade Lux Lewis, and many more.

In the 1920s and 30s the blues developed into two popular piano styles, barrelhouse and boogie-woogie, which were primarily performed by traveling musicians who played at "barrelhouses" and "rent parties," passing on their knowledge and skills as they went.

The pianos were of such poor quality that the pianists often had to adapt their playing styles to accommodate out-of-tune notes and broken strings. This gave rise to the term "honky tonk" to describe these instruments. Most modern keyboards will have a piano patch with that name.

Blues was then taken up by the swing bands of the 1940s, who commercialized the music and toured it around the country. The bandleaders included Benny Goodman, Count Basie, and Glenn Miller, whose hit tune "In The Mood" is still popular today.

The 1950s saw a change of direction. With the invention of the electric guitar in 1948 and changes in American society, a generation of rebellious teenagers was eager for something new. They latched on to rock'n'roll, an exciting sound that emerged from the South. Its risqué lyrics and blend of blues, boogie-woogie, and country & western signaled a new era in the history of the blues.

The jukebox and television helped to spread the music to an international audience and gave birth to huge stars, including Elvis Presley, Bill Haley, Chuck Berry, and piano legends Jerry Lee Lewis and Little Richard. Blues formed the foundation of jazz, soul, gospel, rock, and funk, and continues to influence music today.

The pieces in this unit focus on the blues chord sequence in several keys and provide a knowledge of the various chords, scales, basslines, rhythms and riffs used in the different styles covered. The examples focus on the unique problems associated with co-ordinating the left and right hand, and the unit closes with a look at improvisation.

The 12-bar blues chord sequence is the standard form of the blues. The Roman numerals show the relationship between the chords in any key, as explained in Unit One. The sequence can easily be broken down into three four-bar sequences. This will help you memorize it. In "Lucky Number 12" the sequence is written out in C major. Inversions of the chords are used to make it simpler to move from one to another, against a simple walking bassline in the left hand.

Practice the individual chord shapes first, making sure to place your thumb on the lowest note of the chord and your little finger on the highest. This will keep your hand balanced.

Then practice changing from one chord to another. Give yourself enough time, at least half a beat, so that you can land cleanly on beat one of the next bar. Once you feel comfortable with this, play along with the CD. If you get lost, listen to the bass; this will get you back on track.

The great thing about chord symbols is that it's up to you how you play them, so try starting with a different inversion of C7 and let that dictate what follows. Move to the nearest F7 and carry on the sequence in the same way. It's best to make small moves when changing chords rather than jumping.

Transpose the blues sequence into other keys. This will give you flexibility, especially when working with singers, and build up your chord knowledge.

Example 2.1, "Lucky Number 12"

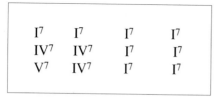

RHYTHM AND THE BLUES

We can't talk about the blues without talking about rhythm. A key element of any musical style is the beat or the groove, which makes it unique.

With blues and jazz there are two ways of sub-dividing the beat. We can play straight eighths, which means that the quavers are played evenly, with the same amount of time given to each, or we can play "swing" eighth-notes, where the first eighth-note is longer than the second. Traditionally this was written out as a dotted eighth-note/sixteenth-note rhythm. However if we are

going to play this accurately it wouldn't sound right. By dividing a quarter-note into a triplet and giving the first beat two triplets and the second beat one we arrive at "swing feel" (also known as "triplet feel").

Nowadays it's sufficient to write a tune out using quavers but indicate at the top of the music that you want it played in swing feel.

Swing Quavers

The triplet is the foundation of the blues and jazz feel.

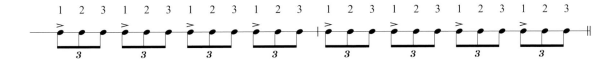

Clap the 1 and the 3 while counting the 123 out loud. You are now clapping in swing (triplet feel).

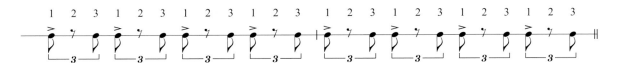

When you see this instruction, play the eighth-notes in swing feel.

Traditionally, jazz and blues are written out using this rhythm, but you should play with a swing feel.

When you see this instruction, you should play the eighth-notes exactly as written.

BLUES AND THE PIANO **UNIT TWO/33**

SYNCOPATED FIGURES

Now that we've grasped the 12-bar chord sequence and have an understanding of the blues feel, let's get swinging. We are going to play some simple syncopated figures in the right hand against a steady left-hand walking bass. Before you play along with the CD, look at the different rhythms in bars one, two, and nine, and try clapping them or tapping them out on your knees.

Tap four steady quarter-notes with your left hand and the syncopated rhythms in your right.

Don't worry if you don't get this at first; co-ordination is key to keyboard playing, so it's worth persevering.

Once you've mastered the tune, try switching the rhythms around in the right hand to make up your own blues.

Example 2.2, "Swing Thing"

THE BLUES SCALE

Now we are going to turn our attention to melody. In order to do this we need to look at the blues scale, the essential scale used in this music.

The blues was originally a vocal form of music accompanied by guitar. Both these instruments have the ability to bend notes, raising or lowering the pitch by small increments. This is a luxury that we don't have on the piano.

In order to recreate that sound, pianists introduced "blue"

notes into the scale: these are the flattened third, fifth, and seventh. Notice that the blues scale is a seven-note scale with the second and sixth degrees missing.

Try out the blues scale, paying special attention to the fingering, and then progress to the two-octave and triplet versions once you're ready. The triplet workouts are designed to increase your speed.

Start slowly and gradually increase the tempo.

Example 2.3, The Blues Scale

Scale degrees

Blues scale in C

Eighth-notes

Triplets

Triplet workout 1

Triplet workout 2

REPETITIVE PHRASES

Many blues tunes are built around a repetitive right hand phrase. "Riffin'" emphasizes the relationship between the fifth and flattened fifth in the melody. Be careful to observe the articulation and play the melody with a light bouncy feel.

The walking bass is similar to "Swing Thing," but there are some additional notes from the blues scale in bars four and eight. Chromatic notes—notes outside the key of the piece—are often used to walk between two different chords. Play the bass

as legato (smoothly) as possible; don't worry, you will have to jump occasionally.

In bar 12 there is an extra chord for the last two beats. As we are repeating the sequence, we can use the dominant chord G7 (chord V) to take us back to the beginning. This is generally known as a "turnaround". The second-time bar uses a classic blues ending in the bass. Be sure to memorize this pattern and try it out in other keys.

Example 2.4, "Riffin'"

Barrelhouse is a style of blues piano that came out of the southern states of America in the 1920s, although its roots may be much earlier than that. It was played in the rough bars called "barrelhouses" which were often nothing more than wooden shacks. It is quite a simplistic form of the blues, as the musicians who played it often had little or no formal training. The key characteristics are a repetitive left-hand pattern of open fifths and octaves, which outlines the chord sequence, against a right hand of repetitive embellishments.

The left-hand part in "Barreling Along" has one of the simplest and most popular bass figures, using roots and fifths and roots and sixths (shown as R5 and R6), while the melody is based on thirds that outline the chord shapes. The pick-up notes in bar two use the flat third and fifth of the blues scale to lead up to the third and fifth in the C triad. Notice that they are written as sharps rather than flats. This is purely for ease of reading and to avoid unnecessary accidentals. Practice the bass part separately, making sure you use the correct fingering; keep your hand close to the keys and the rhythm steady as a rock. The chord changes require some jumping around so try this without looking; this way you will get used to the physical distance and free yourself up to concentrate on the right hand.

To play the right-hand phrase in bar three, it helps to roll the wrist slightly.

Example 2.5, "Barreling Along"

We can expand on the previous piece by developing the bassline. By adding a simple repetition of each bass note we get a more bouncy bassline. Don't try to play this smoothly; you need to lift your hand off the keys to play the repeated notes.

The bassline can be heard on CD track 12. Try this bass part against the right hand of "Barreling Along." You may need to experiment with placing the bass in different octaves to see which one gives the best results.

Alternative Left-Hand Pattern

This left-hand pattern is based on the one on the previous page but has a bouncier feel to it. Although it is written out in dotted eighths and 16th-notes, remember to play it as triplets.

BOOGIE-WOOGIE   CD13

Boogie-woogie developed in the 1930s in the urban centers of the United States, including Chicago, Kansas City, and Detroit. Although it retained some elements of the barrelhouse style, with its use of the blues chord sequence, as a solo piano style it is more improvisational than its predecessor. It relies heavily on a percussive left hand of repeated riffs and a right hand of simple patterns that are embellished as the tune progresses.

The first big hit was "Pinetop's Boogie-Woogie" by Pinetop Smith in 1928, which helped put boogie-woogie on the map. Meade "Lux" Lewis had great success with his "Honky Tonk Train," which he recorded many times.

"JM's Boogie" uses a classic boogie bassline built around alternating major and minor thirds, while the right hand has syncopated chords and melodic lines built around sixths. Practice the left hand separately first.

Once that feels comfortable, try out bar two with both hands together before attempting the whole piece. The grace notes or crushed notes in the right hand of bars seven and 11 are a key feature of this style. Although written before the beat, the A-sharp should coincide with the left hand and move onto the B-natural as soon as possible.

Bar ten can be a little confusing. Although it looks as if the G note in the right hand comes before the bass note, remember that the left hand is actually triplet feel, so they should sound together. Always start slower than the tempo indicated and work up to the required speed.

Example 2.6, "JM's Boogie"

Rock'n'roll is a blend of many styles, including rhythm & blues, country & western, boogie-woogie, and gospel. It came about due to the migration of musicians from city to city in the 1950s, which led to them picking up different influences. Although the electric guitar dominated the new music, the piano still played a central role. Two pianists who came to the fore at this time were Jerry Lee Lewis and Little Richard, whose flamboyant playing and stage antics are legendary.

As in boogie-woogie, the left hand plays repetitive percussive figures and the right hand plays licks, embellishments, rolls, and "glisses." As the solo instruments of choice are guitar and saxophone, the piano generally takes on an accompaniment role, with occasional forays into the limelight. To compete with drums and guitar, the piano had to really thump the sound out, so you'll find the right hand driving repetitive rhythms at the top end of the piano.

"Slip Slide" is an introduction to rock'n'roll piano playing. Notice that "straight eights" is written at the top of the music. In the section marked "8va" the right hand part is played an octave higher than written. The word "loco" is a reminder that from there on the part is played as written.

Example 2.7, "Slip Slide"

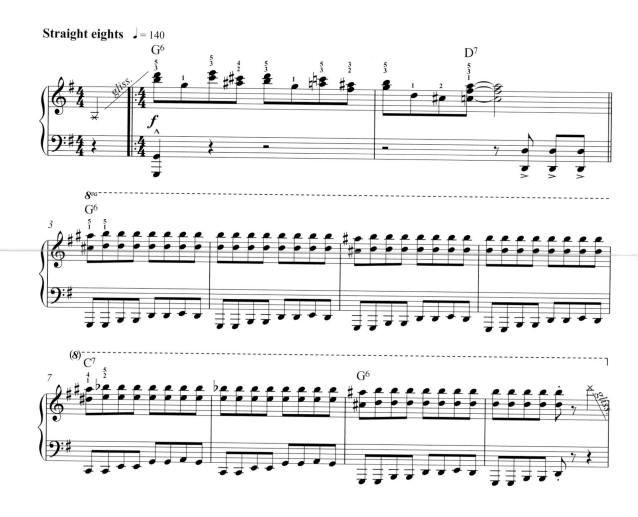

The bass part is based on the notes of a sixth chord—that is root, third, fifth, and sixth. As a general rule, isolate the left hand and practice it with a bouncy feel until it is rock steady. You should be on automatic pilot when you put the two hands together.

The "gliss"—which is short for "glissando," Italian for "sliding"—is synonymous with rock'n'roll, so there are a few thrown in here for good measure. The starting note is given in bars 1, 15, and 17; then you need to run your hand down or up the white notes to land on the next chord in time. This is no mean feat. To prevent serious injury, when doing an upward gliss turn your hand over and use your nails to run up the keyboard. When doing a downward gliss place your thumb under your hand and pull your thumbnail down the keyboard. This may take a bit of getting used to. Try to keep your arm feeling light so that you don't get stuck down in the keys.

Although the 12-bar blues sequence is fundamental to rock'n'roll, some of the players started to open out the form, especially in slower tempos. Fats Domino was one of these guys. His most famous composition, "Blueberry Hill," is in the AABA form used in many "standard" songs.

"Domino's Dance" uses a classic Fats Domino bass figure built on the triads of the chord sequence, with a triplet pattern for the right plus the "roll," a classic rock'n'roll technique.

Notice the new time signature of 12/8. This means that each quarter-note is divided into three eighth-notes. This is just another way to write out swing feel; it works particularly well for this type of tune.

Use a slight roll of the wrist for the bass part, make sure that you keep your hand stretched out so that you can reach the octave each time and jump between the chords changes without looking. The right-hand triplet chords should be steady and even in sound.

The lines written under the notes in bars 9, 10, 13, and 14 mean to roll—that is, to repeat the notes rapidly by rocking the hand from side to side. Octaves and chords sound great when rolled too!

Pro tip

The flat keys of F, B-flat, and E-flat are the preferred choice for sax players, while the sharp keys of E, A, and D are preferred by guitarists. Make sure you practice in all these different keys.

Example 2.8, "Domino's Dance"

BLUES LICKS

CD16

"Copy from one, it's plagiarism; copy from two, it's research."
Wilson Mizner

   In order to sound authentic when playing in a particular style it is essential to have the necessary licks and riffs under your belt. A lick is a short musical phrase and a riff is a repetitive melodic figure. Here is a small selection of blues licks written in the key of C. Don't be afraid to copy your favorite players; it's the best way to learn. Try them out in different keys, try different combinations, expand on what's given, and invent your own.

Pro tip
The best way to get into any style is to listen to as many recordings as possible.

Here is a small selection of left-hand bass patterns covering all the styles we've looked at so far. The blues basslines, examples "a" to "d," and boogie-woogie basslines, examples "h" and "i," should be played smoothly. The rest of the basslines should have a slight bounce to them.

Use these as a starting point for your creativity. You could go back and add them to the pieces you've learnt so far, add some right hand improvisation, or you could make up your own melodies to go with them.

Example 2.10, Bass Patterns

Triplet feel

Blues

Barrelhouse

Left-hand shuffle

Boogie-woogie

Rock'n'roll (straight eights)

Up until now the right hand has been providing the chords. Now it's time to focus on the left hand.

Let's go back to the 12-bar blues sequence in C and transfer the chords to the left hand. As with the right hand, using inversions will help to move the left hand around smoothly. Remember, give yourself time to change chords, at least half a beat so you can land on the next chord cleanly.

The rhythmic variations (CD track 19) are written on one chord, but play them over the whole sequence. This type of left-hand part is used when accompanying, or "comping," a singer or soloist.

Pro tip

"Comping," from the word "accompanying," is an important keyboard skill. Try to provide some rhythmic impetus without getting in the way.

Example 2.11, "Lucky Number 12" Left Hand

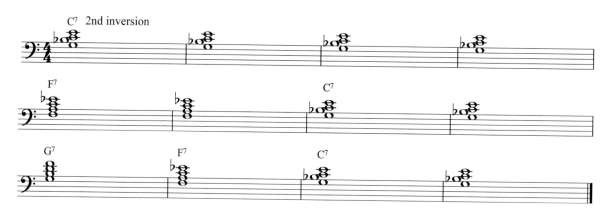

Rhythmic variations

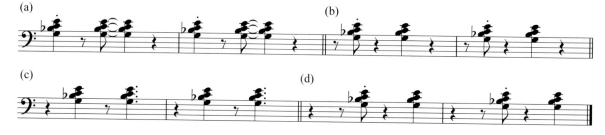

Soloing or improvisation—making it up as you go along—is a core component of jazz and blues.

"Riffin' Two" is a repeat of the earlier tune, with the right-hand melody played an octave higher to accommodate the left-hand chord shapes. There are some "free" bars given with "note boxes." These boxes include note suggestions for improvisation. Familiarize yourself with the notes first before starting.

If you feel stuck and don't know what to play, try using some of the rhythms from the original melody and applying them to the note boxes. You can also leave the left hand out and focus on your right hand only.

We primarily use arpeggios and scales to improvise with. If you listen back to the great players like Louis Armstrong and Fats Waller, who were at the forefront of jazz in the 1930s, you can hear them outlining the chord sequence with these techniques. The note boxes in "Riffin' Two" only use three of the four chord tones.

Try the tune again using all four chord tones to improvise with. Don't get stuck in one place. Remember, you have the whole of the keyboard at your disposal.

We have looked at the blues scale. Now let's put it into practice. Using the 12-bar blues sequence from "Riffin' Two," but discarding the melody, try improvising over the whole sequence with the blues scale. You may find that some notes work better than others, depending on which chord you're playing. Start with one or two notes of the scale and gradually introduce the others as you go along.

Example 2.12, "Riffin' Two"

RHYTHMIC PHRASES

Improvisation is not just about notes; it's about rhythmic invention too. Here are some rhythmic figures for you to try out.

The first example takes a simple figure and shifts it by half a beat to create rhythmic displacement. This is a good trick to have up your sleeve. The subsequent examples use quarter notes, triplets, and off-beats. Try displacing these to see what you get.

It's a good idea when trying out rhythms to start out by tapping first, then play them using a single note, and then apply the scale notes.

Be creative; try to come up with as many different ideas as you can. Your ear is paramount in improvising; if it sounds good then it is good!

Example 2.13, Rhythmic Phrases

Triplet feel ♩ = 100

Rhythmic displacement

Quarter-notes

Triplets

Off-beats

MIXOLYDIAN MODE

You should be really familiar with the sound of the blues scale by now. It's time for a new scale, or rather a "mode." If you look at the diagram of the C major scale there are seven different chords that come out of it. Let's just look at chord V, G7. If the chord comes from the scale, then the scale must fit the chord; that's the theory behind using scales to improvise.

If we take the notes of the C major scale but start on G, we end up with a pattern of whole steps and half-steps that is the fifth "mode" of the major scale; it is called the Mixolydian mode. These scales originated in ancient Greece and are used extensively in jazz. The pattern is: whole step / whole step / half-step / whole step / whole-step / half-step / whole step (tone / tone / semitone / tone / tone / semitone / tone).

You can build the Mixolydian mode on other roots, sticking to the same pattern of whole and half steps. The Mixolydian modes for C7 and F7 are written out here. Let's try the 12-bar again using these new scales.

Be sure to put into practice all the techniques that you've learnt in the previous few pages.

Theory tip
In the Mixolydian mode the seventh note is flattened from the major scale. This scale can be used to improvise on a dominant seventh chord.

Example 2.14, Mixolydian Mode

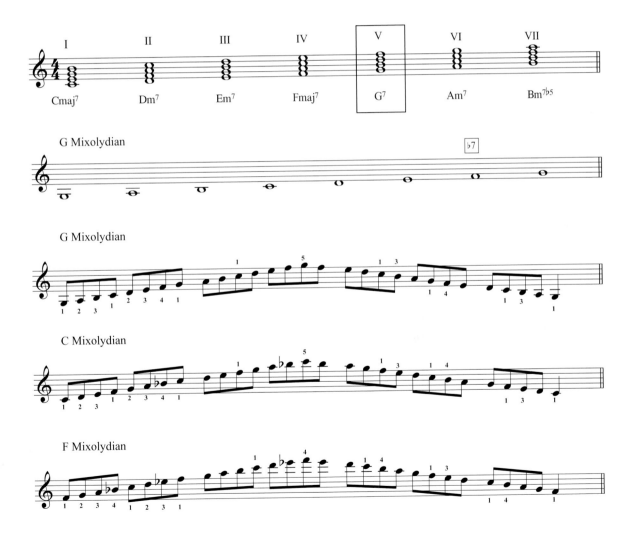

MINOR BLUES

Perhaps the most famous of all minor blues tunes is George Gershwin's 16-bar blues, "Summertime." Minor blues tunes tend to be slower, due to their melancholy nature.

Let's look at some of the theory behind the minor blues. In a minor key, chords I and IV are minor and chord V is major. (Look at the scale at the top and you will see that the seventh degree of the scale is sharpened, compared with the seventh degree of the natural minor scale, to make this happen; the sharpened seventh is always shown with an accidental.)

The minor blues chord sequence is exactly the same as for the major blues. However, there are many variations to this sequence, which we will take a look at later.

Practice the chord shapes first and then try the minor blues scale.

Example 2.15, Minor Blues

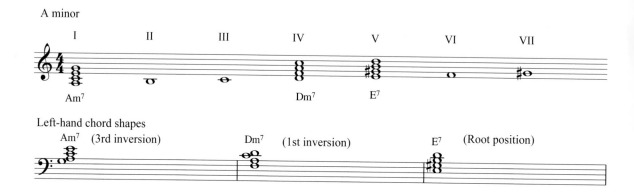

Here are some scale examples that will help you play the melody
of the next piece, "Lonesome Blues." Again, the triplet workouts
are intended to help you build up speed.

Eighth-notes

Triplets

Triplet workout 1

Triplet workout 2

MINOR 12-BAR

"Lonesome Blues" uses the standard 12-bar sequence in the key of A minor. A minor is the relative minor to C major, so there is no key signature.

Keep the left-hand chords punchy and the right hand lyrical. When you've mastered the tune, try improvising over the chords.

Use the A minor blues scale and the left-hand pattern of "Lonesome Blues." If you find it too difficult to keep the left hand rhythm going while improvising, just use whole notes for the chords. Watch out for the straight eights feel!

Example 2.16, "Lonesome Blues"

DORIAN MODE

So far we've looked at the blues scale and the Mixolydian mode. But when it comes to minor chords, we need a new mode, the Dorian mode.

The chord built on the second degree of any major scale is always minor. Working back we see that the Am7 chord comes from the G major scale. By playing the notes of that scale, starting on its second degree, we arrive at the Dorian mode.

Apply the same theory to the Dm7 chord and you'll get D Dorian, which is made up of the notes of the C major scale, but starting on the second degree. The pattern for the Dorian mode is this: whole step / half-step / whole step / whole step / whole step / half-step / whole step (tone / semitone / tone / tone / tone / semitone / tone).

You can add these modes to your improvising.

Example 2.17, Dorian Mode

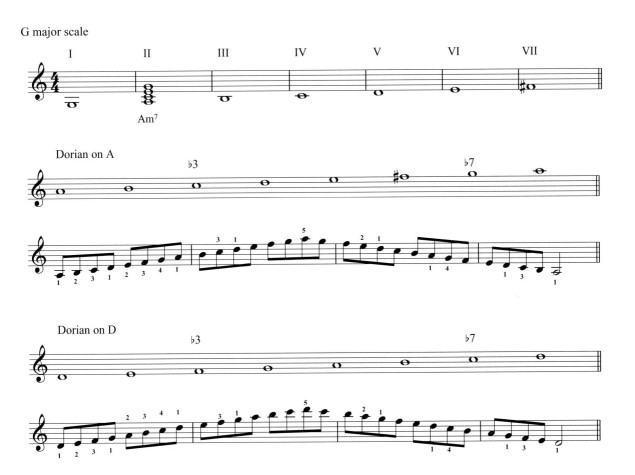

MIXOLYDIAN MODE

The E7 is a dominant chord and therefore the Mixolydian mode applies. As you can see, the more chords we have, the more scales we need to know.

By taking these simple chord sequences and playing them in other keys you will gradually build your chord knowledge.

Example 2.18, Mixolydian Mode

DEVELOPING THE BLUES

CD21

You don't have to be restricted to the standard form of the blues. There are many ways to vary the sequence. A blues sequence can be anything between eight and 24 bars long. Some classic tunes, like Bill Withers' "Ain't No Sunshine" and Herbie Hancock's "Watermelon Man," use the blues in its eight-bar and 16-bar forms respectively.

"Lonesome Blues Two" has 16 bars with some additional chords in bar five and a change to the sequence in bars ten and 11. This has a knock-on effect when it comes to the improvisation.

Bars five and six have what is commonly known as a II-V-I pattern in the key of D minor. A7 is the dominant chord of D preceded by Em7, which is the second in the key of D minor. This harmonic device is ever-present in music and many of the songs from the 30s and 40s are based on this three-chord cycle. Bar ten has an alteration to the chord, where the dominant seventh is raised a half-step (semitone) falling to the dominant chord in bar 11.

Example 2.19, "Lonesome Blues Two"

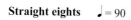

So far the styles we have considered have been based firmly on the piano. But by the middle of the 20th century, alternative keyboards were becoming available. The first of these was the Hammond organ, which gained a foothold in the market, for both sacred and secular purposes, in the 1940s. Then, in the 1950s, the Hammond acquired the "percussion" feature, which inspired a clutch of musicians who would define soul-jazz, spearheaded by Jimmy Smith.

Electric guitars were by now commonplace, and the first electric pianos began to appear. Harold Rhodes' invention suffered what may have been the longest gestation of any instrument. In 1949, he designed and built an electric piano using cylindrical metal rods called "tines" as a sound source, but it would take until 1965 before the instrument went into production as the Fender Rhodes. In the meantime, the organ and jukebox company Wurlitzer had

developed and marketed its own electric piano, using vibrating steel reeds as a sound source. It went on the market in 1954. The German manufacturer Hohner, meanwhile, developed first the Pianet electric piano, launched in 1962, and then the Clavinet, in which strings are struck by rubber hammers. Introduced in 1964, it was quickly seized upon by musicians like Stevie Wonder who took it into funky areas undreamed of by its creators, who saw it as a substitute for the stately clavichord.

Naturally, the new instruments affected the way musicians played and the way they wrote. The world of jazz, which can still be puritanically dismissive of electric instruments, first encountered the electric piano in 1966 when Joe Zawinul used a Wurlitzer when recording his own tune "Mercy, Mercy, Mercy" with saxophonist Cannonball Adderley's band.

Zawinul had first come across the Wurlitzer when he was working with singer Dinah Washington on a tour with the soul legend Ray Charles. Charles had given the Wurlitzer its first hit in 1959 with "What'd I Say."

Soul was a blend of elements derived from the blues and gospel music, resulting in a music that had pop appeal, rhythmic drive, and harmonic sophistication, while retaining the directness and earthiness of the blues. One of its centers was Detroit, home to the Motown record label, which had absorbed a wave of migration of black workers from the South in the first half of the 20th century. Meanwhile, there was plenty of soul still in the South. The Stax label, based in Memphis, Tennessee, had its own distinctive soul sound. In both cases, the music was created by house bands: organist Booker T. Jones and The MGs in the case of Stax; pianists Joe Hunter and Earl Van Dyke and The Funk Brothers in the case of Motown. Initially the instruments used would have been piano and Hammond organ. Later electric pianos found their way into the studios and quickly became associated with the soul sound.

Writers and artists such as Marvin Gaye, Stevie Wonder, and Booker T. Jones took to the new sounds with great enthusiasm. Gaye and Wonder were both true multi-instrumentalists. Gaye first worked for Motown as a session drummer, before becoming a singer and songwriter. Wonder turned just about everything he touched to gold, finding a natural, vibrant musicality on drums and keyboards, not to mention harmonica.

Unit Three starts with some style examples based on music from this period. It continues with the gospel, soul-jazz, funk, and reggae music that was in a state of constant development through the 1960s.

The Wurlitzer electric piano is absolutely perfect for riffing in the mid range, an octave either side of Middle C (known as C4 in MIDI notation). But one reason it never quite took off with the jazz fraternity is that as soon as you go higher on the keyboard the sound thins out considerably, making projection on a solo well nigh impossible. The sound is less interesting at the top too: it loses the springy rubber-band element that makes the mid and bass so appealing.

This Wurly part, modeled on Gaye's "I Heard It Through The Grapevine," uses a riff on D minor (though the original is in E-flat minor), voiced in open fifths. This is an inventive sound that the instrument rather dictates, because with a third in the chord also, the sound would become bottom heavy. This parallel fifths

technique is the same that guitarists use in power chords; put in the third and it becomes a stodgy mess.

On your keyboard, dial up a Wurlitzer patch. It'll probably have a tremolo option that fluctuates the volume. (That's definitely a tremolo, not a vibrato—a fluctuation in pitch—as the front panel of the Wurly erroneously suggests.) The tremolo was a plus point with the Wurly, as was the fact that you could pick up its 64-key carcass without causing yourself a hernia.

The move to the B minor chord in bar seven is a surprise, and something that Motown tracks became increasingly fond of. In the last four bars, check out the difference between the Gmaj7 chord, and the G7 chord. The G7 flattens the F-sharp, preparing for a return to D minor home base.

Example 3.1, "Curly Wurly"

Come the 1970s, things were changing at Motown. There was an air of experimentation that reflected the social and political climate, and the musical language used to express the spirit of the times was in a state of constant expansion.

This piece is an echo of Marvin Gaye's "What's Going On." The major seventh chords that the example uses in bars one and five give an air of relaxation that flies contrary to the meaning of the song, as does the laidback groove. Played on piano, the whole groove is present in the moving bassline and the articulation of the chords in the right hand. Try to make the interplay between the hands precise but not pushed; and as the rhythm stays the same throughout, keep it steady.

The B-flat ninth chord (Bb9) in bars four and eight needs some explanation: you arrive at a ninth chord by adding the second/ninth degree of the scale to a chord. Here a B-flat seventh chord has a C added to the mix, so the chord is described as a B-flat ninth. In function it is the same as a B-flat seventh. The sound is even more open in this written voicing as the third (D) is left out. The final chord adds a ninth (F) to the E-flat major seventh chord, making a major ninth chord.

If you thought the move to B minor in the previous piece was unusual, here the move to IV minor (a minor chord built on the fourth degree of the E-flat major scale) in bar nine is a killer emotional twist; coupled with the string line, the angst of the subject matter makes itself felt.

Example 3.2, "Changing Times"

Stevie Wonder had learned a huge variety of instruments in the "Snakepit," the colloquial name for Motown's studio. By the early 70s he was creating his own vocabulary of sound. One of his compositional inspirations stems from the blues feel, if not the harmonic form, and this piece, modeled on "Living For The City," has a classic blues riff at its heart. Then it shows another side; the time signature flips to 3/4, and the descending chromatic bassline twists through a succession of chords, one of which needs explaining.

The Eb° stands for an E-flat diminished chord, a chord that is made up of a stack of minor thirds. In this case the E-flat is the root, and F-sharp, A, and C are the components of the chord. A

diminished chord is a transit point in the same way as a seventh chord, wanting to resolve counterclockwise on the Circle Of Fifths. In fact if you were to take the Eb° and put an F root underneath it becomes an F7b9 chord, which is an F seventh with a flattened ninth (see Figure 1). This naturally wants to go home to B-flat.

The first eight bars of the piece skirt around the G-flat of the original. For Stevie Wonder, G-flat major and E-flat minor were comfortable keys; for the rest of us mortals, they can be a struggle to read, let alone play. You might notice that in the 3/4 section some of the bass notes do not match the description of the chords. All will be explained over the page.

Dial up a Rhodes sound and swim around in tremolo.

Example 3.3, "Snakepit Life"

FIGURE 1

(the F# is re-spelt Gb)

MORE CHORDS

Triads with a different bass note are often expressed as "slash" chords, as in the examples here. The slash denotes something over something else, the first chord being a G over an F. When you see a slash chord, play the chord in the right hand and just the bass note in the left. Sometimes the slash chord will be an inversion of a chord, as in the C/E; sometimes it will have a completely unrelated bass note. The really weird ones are things like an E/E♭ or a D/E♭.

The next batch of chords are minor ninths; in the same way as you can transform sevenths into ninths, minor sevenths can have the ninth added to great effect. It makes the harmony even sweeter. In the right hands, and Stevie Wonder is a case in point, the ninth provides an almost mystical other-worldliness. Where would a track like "Visions," from *Innervisions*, be without the ninth chords? There is a variety of voicings here.

Lastly, there are a few diminished "broken chords" as they can be a good way of keeping mobile in the harmonic sense and in the rhythmic sense. Play them slowly, then gradually increase the speed.

Notice there are only three types of diminished chord, in essence. By the time you've done C, C-sharp, and D, you've arrived at E-flat which has the same notes as C. Break up the last G-sharp diminished chord for yourself, using the same fingering principles, avoiding thumbs on black notes.

Example 3.4, Slash Chords, etc

If you want to put into practice all the theory of the last page, what could be better than to dip your toes once more into the harmonic world of Stevie Wonder? Around the time of *Music Of My Mind* and *Talking Book*, the Rhodes was taking over as the core keyboard instrument on the rhythm track. Certainly there were synths and Clavinets, but the Fender Rhodes was the choice for getting up close and personal.

Hinting at "Superwoman" and the overplayed "You Are The Sunshine Of My Life," this piece includes the ninths, slash chords, diminished chords, and general harmonic completeness that characterize Wonder's output in the early 1970s. The use of

"surprise" chords such as the E/F♯ in bar ten makes for great mobility; you can explore flat-side then turn sharp-side at the flick of a wrist. Rhythmically, the example includes at bars six and seven an end of phrase punctuation that was typical of the time, but which sounds a bit cute to 21st-century ears.

The chords at bars 10 and 11 are the kind of sequence that would get used for almost a complete chorus on "Don't You Worry 'Bout A Thing." And the use of a chromatically shifting triad over a fixed pedal bass would form the intro to "Too High."

So the moral of this page is this: if you want to understand the way chords work, look to Stevie Wonder's 70s albums.

Example 3.5, "Wonderful Harmony"

One technique that gives the piano immense accompanying weight is the depth of the bass end, particularly when played in low octaves. In church that's just what you need to inspire a congregation to sing their hearts out, and the sound spread from church to gospel records to mainstream soul styles as a natural progression.

The spirit of Thomas A. Dorsey, pianist with among others Bessie Smith and Ma Rainey, has been passed on to more modern players such as Billy Preston and Oleta Adams. Gospel style is as strong an influence on young musicians as ever, and many are the piano players who, to use Carla Bley's words, "grew up in church."

The up-tempo roaring celebratory gospel form illustrated here can be heard in the work of Mahalia Jackson (with a young organist called Billy Preston in tow). She was an extraordinary singer who crossed gospel with an increasing involvement with jazz, culminating in a collaboration with Duke Ellington.

Example 3.6, "Gospel Celebration"

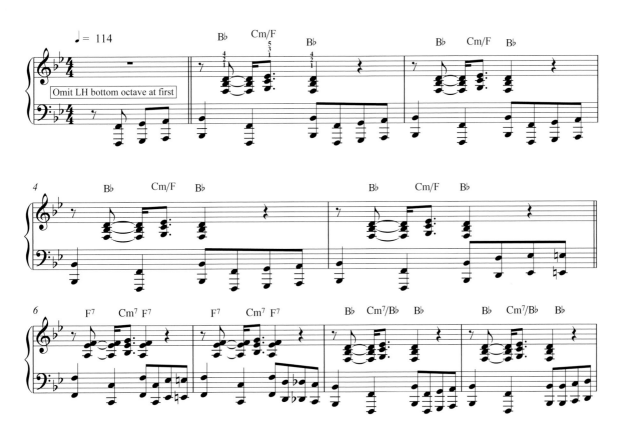

continued on next page

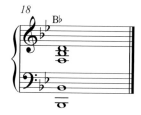

This piece looks a bit scary in terms of handfuls of notes at speed, but don't be afraid. To learn the notes, leave out the bottom notes of the left hand; you'll need to work up to the stretch of an octave. The good news is that once you've learned one bar, the rest is very similar, just turning the progression through a blues-related set of chords (I, V, and IV).

Watch for the octave right-hand run; yes octaves abound in the right hand also, notching up the power. Compare bars 14/15 played single-note, then in octaves. There is no match for sheer bravado. But it does mean having to practice C major octave scales, using first and fifth fingers with a loose wrist. The only tension should be in the fingers.

After a while your strength will build enough to play the piece as written, with rhythmic exuberance.

This piece features the other side of gospel, the slow sustained 12/8 ballad style. Try this with an organ sound, preferably a Hammond patch or software tonewheel clone. If you're lucky there might be a split patch where the right-hand end is glittery and full of the upper harmonics present on a Hammond, and the left hand is more muted in an accompanying role. Play the grace notes as written but also add your own embellishments wherever possible.

The drama of the genre is present in the use of diminished chords to heighten the tension before resolving. The IV–I (F–C) conclusion is quite at home in church; it's an ancient device called a "plagal" or "Amen" cadence. A cadence means two chords in succession, normally the final two in a piece or

section. The plagal cadence has been used in choral music since the 16th century. Draw that bar out as long as possible, making sure that you have the Leslie effect engaged. This simulates the Leslie revolving speaker that is to Hammond as peaches are to cream. Probably the modulation wheel will again be pressed into service to turn this on. It's crucial where you switch the Leslie in, too early and you arrive before the musical point you're trying to heighten, too late and it sounds flat.

Gospel organists slide around the instrument at breakneck speed, probably because the light touch of the keyboard encourages fast finger movement; the 16th-note passages give only a small glimpse of what's possible in the fills/soloing department.

Example 3.7, "Peaches And Cream"

Here's quite a different beast, a funk groove that sits best on one particular instrument, the Hohner Clavinet.

James Brown has a lot to answer for. He was probably responsible for kicking off the whole funk style, which was later taken up by Sly Stone and his bass player Larry Graham. Then came George Clinton of Funkadelic, the jazz-funk fraternity, and Prince. (If you're wondering where Stevie fits in, he gets a page to himself overleaf.)

Nothing can quite prepare you for the experience of playing a Clavinet: the feel of the vibrating string, the extremely short travel of the keys, and the damped guitar-like funk of the sound itself mean it's hard to take your hands away. Even a synth patch demands playing in a very precise and disciplined way. Fistfuls of notes don't do it; the whole upper end of the keyboard doesn't do it; smooth legato passages certainly don't do it. What works is short, staccato notes in the two octaves around middle C, split between the hands, sparingly arranged (often in fourths in the right hand), and played accurately but with feel.

This piece is notated an octave above where it will sound, for ease of reading. Most synths program their clav sounds so that you naturally play the low register. In a band context the range of the clav sits between bass and guitar, weaving around both.

Example 3.8, "Funky Clav"

Stevie Wonder needs a page to himself, because "Superstition" is probably the best known Clavinet part ever to have hit the airwaves. He piled up his rhythm parts for drums and bass but he also stacked up his keyboard parts. The resultant mesh of two or maybe three Clavinet parts on that track grooves like crazy, helped by the swing feel of the 16th-notes, meaning that instead of playing the 16th-notes as a straight pair, play them as a triplet group of eighth-note/16th-note as indicated.

The style is similar to the previous example, with the second note in the left-hand part, the E, played as short as it will sound. This is often referred to as a "choked" note and serves to drive the rhythm but does little for the pitch side of things. For the bridge section at bar six the chords are sustained for once, and

a look at bar eight announces the arrival of a new chord on the block, and a funky customer it is too. We have seen this shape before in the right hand of a 13th chord. (See Figure 2.)

In the right hand the F13 has the tritone and a fourth above it. Change the root note in the bass from an F to a B, however, and things change. Suddenly the E-flat is D-sharp, the third of a B7 chord, the A is the seventh and the D on top is the sharpened ninth. So you have a chord, B7♯9, that contains effectively a major third (between B and D-sharp) and a minor third (between B and D). That's the great blues crunch. Try voicing a 7♯9 chord on other roots to get your fingers used to finding it. Start with the E7♯9 that is the last chord here.

Example 3.9, "Choked Up"

continued on next page

FIGURE 2

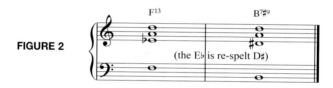

(the E♭ is re-spelt D♯)

The rhythmic syncopation or offbeat activity makes a clav part hard to read, so it's probably best to listen first to the CD to make sense of the 16th-note rests and pushes. The first two bars sit happily over a straight D7 harmony while bars four to six incorporate various funk elements borrowed mostly from guitarists. The half-step/semitone phrase in the right hand on beat two of bar four is the equivalent of a fret slide on guitar. The chord on beat four of the same bar has an unlucky name: if you add the sixth note of a scale to the seventh chord you arrive at a 13th. In this case it's an F13, which is an F7 with a D at the top.

Bar six has the same thing based on E, with the sixth, a C-sharp, on top. Take away the root and you're left with an angular sound, the D and G-sharp forming an interval called a "tritone." The tritone, made up of four whole steps or tones, is an uncomfortable interval. In early church music it was forbidden and was called "diabolus in musica": the devil in music. That's unsettling enough, but add the fact that the interval between the D and the top note C-sharp is a stark major seventh, and you're left with what is on paper a pretty unpleasant combination of notes. Put the root E back in, though, and it all makes sense again in a crisp sort of a way.

Keyboards have a proud place in the history of reggae. Lee "Scratch" Perry and Bob Marley & The Wailers used keyboards in their "dub" productions. In the case of Bob Marley, he often took a keyboard player on tour, either Bernard Touter or Jean Alain Roussel, playing organ or sometimes Rhodes electric piano.

While it may look technically simple, a two-handed "skank," as it's called, is exacting in its loose/tight, relaxed/tense, worry/don't worry mind game. The secret is to play, not think, and listen to things going on around you while keeping perfect time.

The pattern on the top set of staves, labeled Rhodes, is the one to concentrate on. The touch sensitivity of the Rhodes is an advantage when compared to the Hammond in the same situation, the left hand being suggestive rather than forceful, the right hand emphasizing the first chord of each pair.

The second stave is a Clavinet part that introduces a bassline figure. The challenge here is to keep the right hand very steady indeed while playing 16th-notes with the left hand.

You'll notice this piece doesn't have an ending. Just keep on going round and vary what you're doing ever so slightly by shifting the voicing or leaving out the occasional bar. Time will start to take on another meaning.

Example 3.10, "Top Skanking"

If "Superstition" is the prime example of a Clavinet track, "Green Onions" has to be a contender for best-known Hammond track. Booker T. & The MGs were the house band in the Stax studio, equivalent to the Funk Brothers at Motown, but with a very different sound. Whereas Motown meant broad palette productions, the soul of Stax was pared down to a cooler sound. That's reflected in the Hammond, as well as the overall production, of "Green Onions."

To play this piece you need a fairly flat Hammond patch with little top-frequency activity. Expressed in terms of the Hammond drawbars that control the levels of the various harmonic frequencies in the sound, you need an 8'/4' combination. The quavers are swung, and as with clavinet, it's what you leave out that makes the difference. The third is often omitted in these voicings.

Example 3.11, "Know Your Onions"

Bars five and six are a variation based on the V tonal area (E), and bars seven and eight are a variation based on the IV tonal area (D). It's probably worth playing spot the difference, as the patterns are not just a transposition of the original (I) patterns in bars one to two or three to four.

The key to the groove here is the rocking of the octave movement in the right hand. The sixth chords also need a mention. Why, if there's a sixth in the chord, isn't it called a 13th? The reason is that there's no seventh in the chord, so it has to be a G6 rather than a G13, which always has the seventh included. Same goes for the F6/9 chord in the first two bars: no seventh means that adding the sixth (D), and the ninth (G), results in what can be called an F "added" 6/9, if you like.

Example 3.11, "Know Your Onions" *continued*

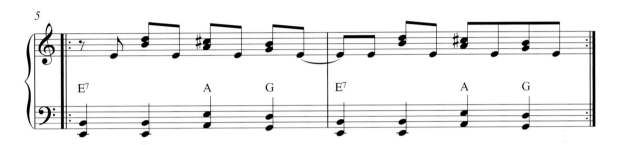

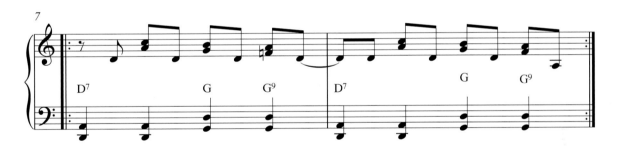

What if you're not reading and working your way through this tutorial, but instead are in a room with a bass player and a drummer, about to settle down to a few hours rehearsal? You could do worse than give the bass player the left-hand part to play, tell the drummer to use his ears, and off you go. Play the tune, then improvise your own phrases the second and third time around.

If you're working on your own, however, play the left hand, which now carries the harmony and the groove, and play the right hand as described above. What notes should you play when improvising? Handily enough, one of the first scales we looked at, the A natural minor/Aeolian mode, works fine for bars one to four. The next six bars can be covered using the Dorian

mode, which, as we saw in Unit Two, is D to D on the white notes. It differs from the natural minor in that it has a major sixth, so if it was based on A there would be an F# not an F. The Dorian on D is written out: it's the mode that underpins much of the "cool" jazz of the late 1950s and 60s. To get it working in E, just take it up a tone, which is the second of the scales illustrated.

You might find that bars one to four sound a bit flat just using white notes, so the obvious first port of call for some blues spice is the addition of the note E-flat. That's the flat fifth of A, and used either as an eighth-note passing note or landed on for a length of time, it should work fine. In the end your ears are the final arbiter. The feel and sound for this piece should be the same as for are the previous example.

Example 3.12, "A La Mode"

Billy Preston was present at one of the crucial periods of pop history, the break-up of The Beatles. The single "Get Back" is unusual in several respects. It's a Beatles single with Preston on Fender Rhodes, and it's a single with that rarest of rock/pop attributes, a keyboard solo. Preston, sometimes described then as the "Fifth Beatle," sounds really comfortable with the band. But so he should; as a young star his experience was already vast, and he could certainly handle the pressure of working with star names. His style on "Get Back," blues and rock'n'roll in one happy mix, propels the track to another level.

The trouble with solos is that they're more difficult to read than they are to play and this one is no exception. Again, listen to the CD to pick it up by ear, then check against the written

notes if that feels a more natural process. But it should not be too frightening; it's designed as an extension of the flat-fifth technique on the previous page.

Whether as a grace note or a more lingering visitor, the flat fifth is star guest at the party, appearing 14 times. The minor third appears in a supporting role (there are just eight of them), which contributes to the general blues tint, helped in no small manner by the left hand, which is pumping a variation of the "Slip Slide" figure from Unit Two.

Call up a Rhodes patch, then practice hands separately to get the left hand solid. Combine hands when you are comfortable, or as comfortable as Billy Preston was on a rooftop above Savile Row, London, in January 1969.

Example 3.13, "Fifth Gear"

By way of reinforcement, here's another G-based tune with an equal abundance of flat fifths and minor thirds, but sounding very different because it's written in the style of Hammond organ master Jimmy Smith. Dial up a Jimmy Smith Hammond sound; there's no top-end action but a hefty dose of Hammond "percussion", an initial attack that emphasizes the third harmonic. It provides that kick to a Hammond note that is envied the world over; it was the reason Smith got involved with the organ at all. The left-hand role is very different: more of a walking bass, something Smith would do with his left hand where others would use pedals.

It's probably worth setting up a split on your keyboard if there's not a pre-programmed patch, so you have smooth left hand and percussive right. Set a split point and assign sounds to areas of the keyboard; probably this will be done in "Combi" or "Performance" mode, but that's entirely dependent upon the manufacturer of your instrument. (CD track 35 features just the drum part for you to play along with.)

Example 3.14, "G Whizz"

Harmonically, the language of this piece is a step up from the blues, with life pretty straight until the approach to the turnaround in bar nine. There the A7 takes the sequence a turn sharper around the wheel before coming back via the E♭7. The actual turnaround in bars 11/12 applies a similar principle by going as far as an E7 before coming back via the A13♭9 and D9. The A chord is quite advanced; including a 7th and a 13th, and a 9th (but flattened) on top. That begins to look startlingly like an F-sharp triad over an A, and you could describe it that way but you wouldn't want to. Suffice to say it's one of those chords that doesn't crop up much in rock'n'roll but is worth knowing about.

Here's one from left field, as an antidote to blues-derived chord sequences, and a taster of things to come. Great changes were under way at the dawn of the 70s. Among them were the first synths capable of playing more than one note at a time: keyboards dedicated to reproducing the sound of an orchestra. Ken Freeman was first into the arena with his string "Symphoniser". The ARP Solina, Elka Rhapsody, and Crumar Multiman were quick to follow. Call it crude, call it lushly unrealistic, the string machine still holds a fascination.

It is time to wallow in a world of chords that are unrelated but somehow make sense to each other in a cod-classical sort of way. The dawning era would aspire to the heights of orchestral music, not only in sound but also in the ambition of the writing. Drama rules, and so this bunch of chords leads ever onwards and upwards, retaining the top note of the previous chord but scrapping everything else, as in the move from bar five to bar six, where the D-flat becomes a C-sharp and provides the glue to hold together a drastic change. (Think where D-flat and A are on the Circle Of Fifths: hardly next door neighbors.)

The voicings are very much keyboard voicings in comparison to the string arrangements to come in Unit Six. They may sound raw, but that's exactly the point. The left-hand movement in bar nine ratchets up the action, in preparation for the big finish and the final flourish on E, the guitarists' key, ready to enter the explosive world of rock.

Example 3.15, "Grand Designs"

Rock keyboard styles hark back in many ways to the blues era in terms not only of directness of harmonic language but also keyboard technique. The pianistic trickery of the likes of Little Richard was used to drive many a rock track in the 1960s and 70s. Although these were primarily the decades of the electric guitar, keyboards were never out of the picture for long; they were able to provide depth and variety in a mix, while the guitar provided the midrange kick and aggression.

Before prog rock and the synth revolution, the instrumentation was limited to piano, electric piano, and organ. The best players had a command of all three: Greg Allman of The Allman Brothers Band; Bill Payne of Little Feat; Garth Hudson of The Band; and Tom Constanten with The Grateful Dead. All had both "percussive" (piano and electric piano) and "sustaining" (organ) instruments.

Aside from organ and pianos, there was the Clavinet, which was pressed into service as a rock guitar substitute, complete with fuzz pedal/wah-wah effects. The principal exponent was Stevie Wonder, on albums such as *Where I'm Coming From* (1971), *Music Of My Mind* (1972), and *Talking Book* (1972).

The roster of rock keyboardists also has to include a number of Britons who pioneered the incorporation of blues into 60s rock/pop music. The London rhythm & blues scene launched many an organ-led line-up, drawing on soul-jazz but adding a blues/rock rawness to the whole affair. Zoot Money, Georgie Fame, Alan Price, John Mayall, and Brian Auger were all partying in the thronged London clubs, purveying dance music with an edge. This cross-fertilising scene spawned many of the rock bands of the late 60s, including Steve Winwood's Traffic.

The Rolling Stones also paid their dues in this club scene; although primarily a guitar-rock band, they expanded their sonic palette with the addition of keyboards, mostly supplied by Nicky Hopkins. His credits read like the ultimate rock A-list: The Beatles, The Kinks, The Who, The Rolling Stones, John Lennon, and Jeff Beck all enlisted his skills before he went to the USA and worked with Steve Miller and Jefferson Airplane. The Beatles' "Revolution" has fine rock'n'roll piano, while Lennon's "Imagine" boasts a legendary keyboard part doubled by Hopkins. His playing on The Stones' *Exile On Main Street* is textbook "keys-in-a-guitar-band" material, while "Gettin' In Tune" on *Who's Next* is exemplary ballad style.

The classic British rock bands that predate heavy metal, such as Led Zeppelin, Deep Purple, Atomic Rooster, and The Nice (with Keith Emerson), all featured examples of the rock Hammond style that took the instrument beyond a jazz setting. Other electric organs flourished, too, including the Farfisa (Pink Floyd's Rick Wright on *The Piper At The Gates Of Dawn*), Vox Continental (The Animals' Alan Price on "House Of The Rising Sun"), and Lowrey (The Band's Garth Hudson on *The Last Waltz*).

Playing organ was certainly one way to be on a level with the sheer volume of live guitar amplifiers. Meanwhile, live or in the studio, piano muscles were hardening; the only way to cut through was to play hard or at the top end where guitarists were fearful to tread.

This unit concerns itself with developing a forceful rocky style, while cutting back on the jazz chord voicings of the previous unit. The sound is strong and open, not clouded with harmonic additions; and octave power in both hands is required more than ever.

Keyboardists can join the rock party if they contribute to the rhythmic drive and add a melodic element at the top end. But be careful: keep it simple or you'll be shown the door. Major chord triads in all their inversions are good, a bluesy seventh is credible, but a major seventh betrays a rounded harmonic knowledge unnecessary in the raw universe of rock. Unless of course it's that sensitive ballad moment in the set, when anything goes.

The solidity of chord movement that underpins the rock style is well demonstrated in "Who Needs Friends?" Chords a fifth away from each other, E-flat, B-flat, and F, turning clockwise around the Circle Of Fifths, keep a sense of purpose without becoming too fancy. Rhythmically, the right-hand triads are to a piano part what the hi-hat is to a drum kit, stating the smallest

practical time subdivision, in this case the eighth-notes. The left hand balances that activity with supportive octave power, resting the hand by shrinking to single lines occasionally.

Build up the muscle and octave stretch gradually, making sure that the wrist remains loose and the forearms are involved as little as possible. The same goes for the right-hand repeated chords. If there's tension in the wrist, two things will happen: you won't be able to keep it going and things will fall apart; and/or the musical feel will be ragged, with the effort you are making reflected in the sound. The hand roles are reversed in the last four bars, giving the right hand a chance to have a stab at a melody.

If the chords are reminiscent of Joe Cocker/The Beatles' "With A Little Help From My Friends," all well and good.

Example 4.1, "Who Needs Friends?"

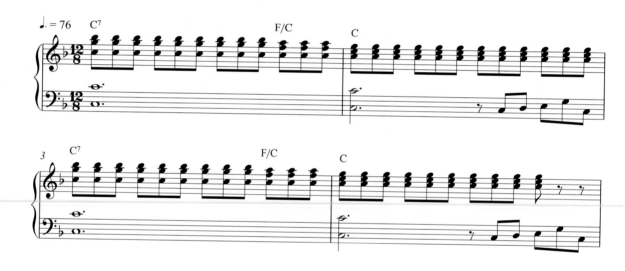

Consider two keyboard players, each living in a place called London, separated by the Atlantic ocean. In London, Ontario, is Garth Hudson; in London, England, Rick Wright. Hudson was keyboard player with The Band; Wright was keyboard player with Pink Floyd. In 1968, both players were busy launching their careers. Hudson moved to the USA to record The Band's *Music From Big Pink*, and Wright was working on *A Saucerful Of Secrets*, the follow-up album to *The Piper At The Gates Of Dawn*.

While neither player would claim to be his band's chief writer, each had a strong musical identity that shaped their sound. Where Hudson is a direct, bluesy player, Wright is more of a colorist, using instrumental texture as well as surprise chords to vary the palette.

"Mid Atlantic" straddles both worlds. The first two bars are firmly anchored in rootsy chords, while the next three bars dip their toes into more adventurous harmonic waters. Even so, bars one and two include a slash chord, the F/G, as well as a handful of right-hand notes, including an octave stretch with a major triad in between. Bars three to five are a more discreet accompaniment passage with the "shocking" major ninth chord pointing the direction to epic.

The three-bar repeated section is unusual but not by the standards of the time. It uses a descending bassline, a favorite device of British bands over the decades. The only difficulty is synchronizing those left-hand dotted notes and ties; just keep the right-hand eighth-notes steady and all will be well.

Example 4.2, "Mid Atlantic"

"Brothers in Crime" owes a debt to The Allman Brothers Band, an outfit that was at its peak on the *At Fillmore East* album of 1971. Forging a blend of country, rock, soul, and jazz that came to be known as Southern rock, brothers Duane (guitar) and Gregg (vocals, Hammond) played long concerts in which tunes could be stretched engagingly for half an hour or so. The tune "Jessica," from Brothers And Sisters, is a treasure chest of pianistic solo ideas played by Chuck Leavell, who has toured with The Rolling Stones, Dr. John, Eric Clapton, and many more. The theme is played in three-part harmony, split between guitar, Hammond, and piano, making an infectious sound. Some call the genre country-rock, which can include bands such as Little

Feat, The Byrds, and even The Eagles and The Doobie Brothers.

What does that mean in keyboard terms? The answer involves the addition of a ninth to a major chord and the omission of the third. In other words, stick a B inside an A major triad, then move it up to the C-sharp at your earliest convenience, either as a grace note or sixteenth-note. In bar ten the C chord boasts a fine example, with the D moving to the E. This device will be back, and will be referred to as "the ninth from the country."

The tune here is split between piano and organ. Try playing each separately, or even together if you can. In the introduction, imagine you are a guitarist and strum/arpeggiate your way through the two chords.

Example 4.3, "Brothers In Crime"

Talk of Chuck Leavell's connections with The Rolling Stones takes us to another player who worked regularly with the band. As mentioned previously, Nicky Hopkins contributed to many a 60s album as a session player, but particularly The Rolling Stones' records.

It's the 1972 classic *Exile On Main St.* that displays his skills most effectively. He sounds completely in tune with the raw, slightly ramshackle, but rootsy feel of that album. The guitar parts even seem to make room for him and the other keyboard players on the album, Ian Stewart and the ubiquitous Billy Preston. It's Hopkins who makes the deepest marks, though: listen to his piano on "Rocks Off," the opening salvo.

Even better, take a look at "Rocks On" here, an attempt

to capture the style of his right hand if not his left. The aim here is to go for maximum drive, the left hand kicking things along with a chunky riff and the right hand almost as active but syncopating across the barline with the imaginary guitar riff. The overall effect is full on rock'n'roll, no holds barred.

Watch the fingering in bars seven to eight: those chromatic sixths are tricky but very much in the style. If you practice a chromatic scale in sixths, that's going to help. A combination of first and second fingers on the bottom note and fourth and fifth on the top should sort things out, coupled with using the same fingers when sliding from black notes to white as in the last two eighth-notes of bar eight. If there's a smudge or two along the way, forget it, it's just rock'n'roll exuberance.

Example 4.4, "Rocks On"

Let's stay with Hopkins but switch bands. Rock music has its less energetic moments, and it's often at these tender times that the piano is called to the fore.

The Who's 1971 album *Who's Next*, was an extraordinary record, made with the help of the ARP and EMS synthesizer companies, but that's another story. Pete Townshend was in top writing and arranging form.

Synths are present on "The Song Is Over," but the star turn is a piano track that shifts gear seamlessly between the lyrical verse and the driving chorus. The contrast between the two is heightened by Townshend taking the more fragile vocal on the verse, handing over to Roger Daltrey on the up-tempo section.

The climax involves piano and lead-line synth, with Nicky Hopkins masterful, building the tension before the track subsides once more.

It's the lyrical section of that song that "Not Over Yet" emulates, keeping a thickish voicing in the left hand, and pulsing with the right hand, with ornamentation in the shape of the triplet 16th-notes. Use the pedal to lend richness, but be careful not to blur the chord changes.

On the subject of chords, as you can see, there are major sevenths and major ninths, all over other bass notes (not the root). And you were promised an easy time with the harmony! It's just that when it comes to the end of a love affair, a Bbmaj7/C is exactly what's required.

Example 4.5, "Not Over Yet"

In the late 1960s and early 1970s there were many pots bubbling away on the stove. If you take a dessert spoonful of country rock, add a half teaspoon of New Orleans funk, and a pinch of jazz, then shake and blend with the vocals of Lowell George, you have the dish known to the world as the band Little Feat.

On keyboards was the redoubtable Bill Payne, one of those players who could make pianos, electric pianos, and organs sound right. It's his intricate, sophisticated use of the Fender Rhodes, honed during his career with Little Feat, that is highlighted in "Heroic Times." The piece is freestanding, which means that the left hand is probably busier than it would be in a band situation, but it has the advantage that it provides a platform for the right-hand displacements to kick off from. These displacements occur when a chord or note is shifted later by a 16th-note as in the first beat of bar two. The result is a fidgety, restless type of edgy, funky rock that refuses to settle down.

"Time Loves A Hero" (1977) is the source material here, though the conclusion refers to another Little Feat tune, "Long Distance Love," from 1975.

Example 4.6, "Heroic Times"

The Allman Brothers Band were not alone in expanding the role of instrumental improvising in rock. In the San Francisco Bay area in the late 60s, a band with links to the multimedia "happenings" and LSD scene was honing its craft under the guiding light of Jerry Garcia. The Grateful Dead are often called a psychedelic band, but for me their sound has more to do with blues and folk than the synth-driven psychedelic wave. Not their compositions, however: they flick through genres faster than shuffling cards, sounding swampy one minute, funky the next, space jazzy the next.

Prior to recording the *Live/Dead* album of 1969, they had recruited keyboard player Tom Constanten to play alongside Hammond organist Ron "Pigpen" McKernan. The two got along famously, although Constanten was never happy on either the

Vox Continental or Hammond, and he left in 1970. The organ track on "St. Stephen," a relatively short track at 6:32, is a study in organ fills around a three-chord riff.

Our pastiche, "St. Vitus," is refreshingly light on left-hand interest; that hand will have to switch in the Leslie effect or operate some tone controls. The right hand plays some riff chords, but it's the second bar of each pair that holds the interest, by single-line filling with 16th-notes.

Experiment with where to switch the Leslie on and off; you need to allow five seconds or so for maximum effect. Many players engage the Leslie to crank up the emotional intensity for a B section in an AABA song form, then switch off for calmer A-section waters.

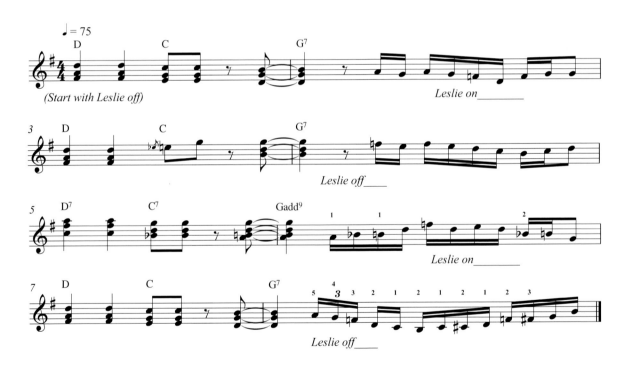

At first glance "Heavy Traffic" also looks a bit light in the left hand, but consider it a base for expansion; you could add a lower octave, you could vary the rhythm, you could add a fifth (D) above it, add a G above that also, or you could leave out a beat occasionally.

"Heavy Traffic," returns us to the theme of hitting things hard in a rock environment. Steve Winwood still enjoys a healthy musical life, touring with Eric Clapton and ducking in and out of the carousel that is the music business. In the days of Traffic, his piano-playing was to the fore, and on tracks such as "Freedom Rider," he showed his skill at power octave right-

hand fills. Traffic followed a similar curve to The Grateful Dead, starting with pop songs then taking on more soloing. By the time of 1970's *John Barleycorn Must Die*, the Traffic sound was fuelled by psychedelia and jazz-rock. It's still rock, though; in this pastiche the right hand is executing almost a drum fill. In fact the last phrase, at bar eight, is a cliché drum pattern that somehow works on piano.

If the underlying chords remind you of Elton John, it's just a reminder that he's an underrated piano player. Repeat this one around and try your own variations; you might like to think of a drum rhythm and transfer it to the keyboard, in octaves of course.

Example 4.8, "Heavy Traffic"

FIFTHS EXERCISE

"Round The Houses" is more of an exercise than a stylistic example. It revolves counterclockwise around the Circle Of Fifths, C–F–B♭ etc, while repeating the eight-bar cycle. That consists of two similar four-bar phrases, the top right-hand melody being shadowed with underneath harmony. In the first four bars the top line starts on the C root note, while at bar five the melody starts on the same C, though this time it's the fifth of the key of F.

The first thing to do is learn the two versions note for note, then transpose the idea around the circle. That way you'll cover all the keys in no time at all. By the time you get to about G-flat, the line will be sounding too low, so take the right hand up an octave at that point and continue round. Change the left hand

one round later, on the B, so that the whole texture isn't transported up at the same time.

When all that's comfortable, it's time to take a few liberties and cut loose with either some variations on the melody/chord movement, or some single-line soloing if that's up your street. Try the blues scale in the right hand and keep the left hand the same; or you could try a left-hand voicing without the root (first inversion) as if there were a bass player. This one exercise could take many months/decades to cover, as the possibilities are limited only by your imagination. (It's a good idea to insert a progression like this into your warm-up routine; it warms up physically and mentally, and it's crucial to cover as many keys as possible.)

It's back to the Clavinet for this one; not an obvious choice for a rock axe, but when Stevie Wonder came of age he liked nothing better than to forge a backing track using Clavinet where guitar might have suited some. After all, open up a Clavinet and inside lurk strings and what looks suspiciously like a guitar neck. Do what guitarists do: overdrive the sound, wah-wah it, or, even better, auto-wah it. The first idea distorts the sound but in a nicely crunchy way, the second sweeps the frequency range, cutting the highs, and the third is an envelope-following filter that automatically sweeps the frequency range, saving the player a lot of physical effort with a foot pedal.

By the early 1970s Wonder was layering up his own rhythm tracks, and the album *Where I'm Coming From* sports a clav track

that hints at what is to come. "Do Yourself A Favor" is full of wah-wah clav with rock attitude. Our example, "Favorite Thing," would sound good with a touch of distortion; the fifths on the answering phrases at bar four and similar would respond the same way as guitar open fifth power chords. Not that guitarists would agree with that statement; usurping their territory, they would say.

Still, if your keyboard lets you in on the effects assignment, it's likely there is an auto-wah/overdrive combination lurking in the insert section, so patch it in and turn it up. (Try playing this piece at pitch rather than the usual Clavinet octave up; it's a bit grumbly occasionally, but nicely gruff at other times.)

Exercise 4.10, "Favorite Thing"

"Angela's Added Ninths" is our final homage to Nicky Hopkins and his relationship with The Rolling Stones. 1973's *Goat's Head Soup* provided an opportunity for Hopkins and Billy Preston to display their skills on their respective tracks. Preston plays some rock Clavinet as well as piano, but Hopkins excels on "Angie," a true ballad with a string arrangement. The right hand ornamentation is full of "ninths from the country" (see Example 4.3, above), this time over minor chords as well as major chords. There are too many to point out. What is worth noting is that joining the ninths from the country are suspended fourths from the country, otherwise known as sus4s.

The idea is very similar; both the ninths and the fourths tend to resolve to the third, so it's a tension/resolution device, the ninths resolving upward, and the fourths downward. I've marked up the first four bars to highlight the use of added ninths and suspended fourths. The penultimate G major chord features both a ninth and a suspended fourth in successive notes, just to reinforce the point.

The left-hand part is kept sparse so as to concentrate on the florid fills, but as time goes on you might want to flesh that out with some eighth-note movement. You could do worse than step through the notes of the triads at a suitable octave: not too low, otherwise mush will ensue.

Pedaling helps the sonority, but again, watch out for blurring; sometimes half-way down on the pedal works better than a full depression.

Example 4.11, "Angela's Added Ninths"

Having relaxed with a ballad, it's time to wake up with "The Long Stretch," a workout from hell. Really it's just a blues, but it's no-holds-barred in terms of octave hammering; not only that, there are notes *inside* the octaves to be played. Actually, that probably makes octave movement easier; any inside smudges contribute to the general energetic melee, provided the outside notes are clean.

The usual recommendations apply: learn each hand separately, left hand first, as that's the most repetitive pattern. The part needs to lodge itself in the back of the brain where it can look after itself semi-automatically. That's not a medically accurate sentence, but there are all sorts of tasks that we perform unconsciously, leaving the front brain to focus on other business. Left-hand bassline activity, if it's not improvised, should be one of those tasks.

Turning to the right hand, take it bar by bar. Usually the second and third fingers will cover the inner grace-note and eighth-note. Where the octave movement is chromatic, cover the top note with a fourth finger if it's a black note, as in bar four, C-sharp and E-flat.

Avoid the temptation to speed up too soon. The piece is marked 108bpm in order to achieve that chunky rock feel; any faster and there's a sense of running away, which is not the rock ethic.

You might have noticed that the form is like a blues, but lasts 16 bars. That's because the E chord and the D chord following last twice as long as in a regular 12-bar. It's just one of the many variations on the blues that have been explored. See Unit Two for more on that.

Example 4.12, "The Long Stretch"

It's one of the most-played guitar riffs of all time. The band virtually wrote the instruction manual for heavy rock and metal. They were, of course, Deep Purple. The riff in question is "Smoke On The Water" from 1972's *Machine Head*. With all that guitarists' adulation, the importance of Jon Lord's Hammond in the band sound is sometimes overlooked.

There are two elements instrumentally and formally in "No smokin'"; organ and guitar are the main protagonists and form-wise there's a riff for a chorus and a guitar chug for the verse. The organ part is not a re-creation of Lord's part, it's a rhythmic counterpoint to the riff itself.

Set up a split on your keyboard (see Unit Six for more on that technique) or use two keyboards to play both instruments, starting with the guitar part. If you don't have a split facility, set up your Hammond sound and play along with the CD, where guitar and drums are eagerly awaiting. The organ part should be pretty easy to read, so how about a spot of soloing?

The third line suggests the E natural minor scale (one sharp in the scale, F-sharp), along with a flattened fifth (B-flat) for blues interest. That's only a starting point. Lord occasionally uses the E minor harmonic scale (the natural minor with a sharpened seventh) for color while soloing. It lends an air of Eastern mystery that is very much of its time.

Be sure to stay away from that on the D chord, though, because the scale's D-sharp introduces a nasty clash with the D. Check bar 11 for those notes.

Example 4.13, "No Smokin'"

The Wurlitzer piano is back for this one, and it's crucial to turn up the "vibrato"—actually tremolo—as we're about to experience the jazz-influenced cool rock of Steely Dan, in particular "Do It Again," their first hit single, from 1972's *Can't Buy A Thrill*. Strange how turning up a tremolo can induce a laid-back mood immediately; that's the nuanced emotional effect of sound. Context matters too: the Latinesque shakers and un-forceful drums cruise along, and the harmony is static also, for a while. Donald Fagen is not a technical player, but a serious groove player. Live, Fagen often sets the groove for the whole band with a four-bar intro. He always sounds most comfortable on Rhodes, but piano, Wurlitzer, and organs of various types are never far away.

In "Logical Dan," the right hand voicings are similar to the open intervals of Unit Three's "Curly Wurly." This time round, though, they are played as fourths rather than fifths. Technically there shouldn't be too many challenges: the important thing is the open voicings and the feel of the groove.

Try soloing over the whole sequence. Natural minor scales rule, particularly in the rising minor chord section at bars nine and ten, where the scale needs to be updated every half bar. Looping bars 9–12 inclusive would be good practice for that section. We've not seen the chord in the last bar before. The B-flat is there as a sharp fifth, even though it's written with a flat. Another name for a chord with a sharp fifth is augmented. To write it as a chord symbol, use a plus sign (+).

Example 4.14, "Logical Dan"

From one purveyor of intelligent rock to another: Frank Zappa. A maverick in the spirit of composer Charles Ives, Zappa was a true bandleader. He expected the best from his bands, and they did not disappoint, mostly because he hired the best players. To do a Zappa audition meant knowing all the songs and sounds without consulting written music. George Duke escaped the audition routine, playing a gig instead to prove his abilities on Rhodes and Minimoog in particular.

Manipulation of the Rhodes sound is the subject of "Digest The Answer." It used to be that the output from a Rhodes was fed into various stand-alone units, such as chorus, phaser, flanger, distortion, or even ring modulator. With modern keyboards the patching is done mostly internally through on-board effects or through an external effects rack unit. To backtrack slightly, the chorus, phaser, and flanger are all pitch or time-modulation effects, the distortion is distortion, and the ring modulator is a device that multiplies the frequencies of two inputs to create very wacky sounds indeed. Have a delve around the effects department of your keyboard and see what's available. Most likely you can hook up two or three effects in a chain, maybe one of the time-modulation variety, and one distortion.

The drum feel is half-time with the snare on beat three, so that needs to be reflected in the keyboard part. You'll notice the return of a couple of "ninths from the country." Other than that, to catch the vibe just experiment with the effects.

Example 4.15, "Digest The Answer"

Just when the reading and technical learning curve seemed to have flattened, along comes a piece that provides a rude awakening. It only just makes it into the rock unit, being on the verge of classical/jazz/fusion rock. The style is reminiscent of The Nice, Keith Emerson's breakthrough band, and the tune should be on Hammond, with a raunchy sound. (CD52 is the bass and drum track.)

Emerson plundered the classical larder for themes, as well as using more contemporary tunes as jump-off points for extensive soloing. "Nice Work If You Can" is influenced by Leonard Bernstein's "America" from *West Side Story* and Dave Brubeck's "Blue Rondo à La Turk." The thing that hits you immediately is the changes of time signature. Don't despair: the bracket over the first bar and subsequent groupings of 12

eighth-notes reveals that the piece is all in 12. So why the changes of time signature then? It's all in the groupings; if a phrase is in pairs of notes it gets notated as /4 as the quarter-note is the pulse. If the phrase is in triplet groupings, the notation needs to be /8 with a 6 or a 12 over it, the dotted quarter-note being the pulse. So the 6/8 bar two has a repeated rhythmic pattern of triplets, while the 3/4 bar three has groups of pairs of eighth-notes. (Time signatures over /4 are referred to as "simple," while those over /8 are called "compound.")

The accuracy with which Emerson could play those tunes is stunning; they're a tour de force, mentally and physically. Check out the 1967 album *The Thoughts Of Emerlist Davjack*, and prepare for "prog rock."

It's hard to imagine the startling impact that the arrival of portable synths must have made. In the 1960s, rooms full of synthesizer modules had been used to shape mainly contemporary/avant-garde electronic music. Suddenly, all-in-one synth keyboards (and some synths without keyboards) were available, and they were capable of being played. Not only could you choose the notes, you could shape the sound you wanted to play those notes with.

Early adopters of the synthesizer included The Beatles on their *Abbey Road* album from 1969. "I Want You (She's So Heavy)" features a Moog white noise effect that builds to the climax, and "Because" contains a brassy, rich Moog sound. This was pre-Minimoog, as was *Switched-On Bach*, the 1968 release by Walter Carlos (now Wendy Carlos). It won three Grammy awards and alerted the world to the arrival of an amazing new technology.

That record was only made possible by the advance of multi-track tape recording, which enabled musicians to record 16 tracks literally side by side and then mix them together. Synthesizers began to be commonly used in studios after 1971, when the Minimoog, the ARP Odyssey/ARP 2600, and the EMS VCS3/Synthi A, found their way into the hands of musicians who were not specialists in electronic music.

Most of the items in this unit are centered on music for synths, so a little knowledge of their workings would be an advantage. There'll be more on that in a moment, but to summarize: a voltage-controlled oscillator (VCO) sends its signal to a voltage-controlled filter (VCF), which sends it on to a voltage-controlled amplifier (VCA), also known as an envelope generator, which shapes the sound in time.

The term VCA needs a touch more explanation. In a VCA, the amplifier section controls the amplitude, or level, of the signal over time: its envelope, in other words. There are four stages to a typical envelope, outlined in the diagram on the left.

The 'A' is the initial *Attack* of the sound, which can be almost instantaneous when you press the key or can come in slowly. *Decay* is the time it takes for the level to fall to that of the *Sustain* portion, which is where it stays while the key is pressed down. When you take your finger off the key, the *Release* parameter determines how long it takes for the sound to die away completely. That's a synthesizer in a nutshell: the pitch and waveforms emerge from the oscillators, their tone is controlled by the filter, and the envelope generator controls their shape in time. Waveforms will be examined in Unit Six.

If that was all there was to synthesis, you might ask what all the

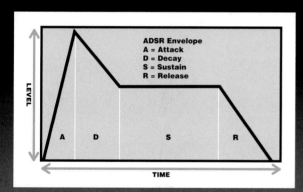

excitement was about. Fortunately, things become more intriguing when you plug (or "patch") things into other things. Controlling the filter tone over time with another envelope generator, applying vibrato to the oscillator by modulating it with a low-frequency

oscillator (LFO), and other such experiments can keep the fingers engaged for hours when they should be practicing the notes.

While all that was happening in the world of technology, the music was responding with an unprecedented rate of change. The sparks of psychedelic rock were igniting and flames were licking around the worlds of rock, classical, and jazz, melting the genres into one another. Blends were made between jazz and rock, classical and rock, jazz and funk, and jazz and world music. Herbie Hancock, Keith Emerson, Joe Zawinul, Stevie Wonder, Rick Wakeman, Jean Michel Jarre, Kraftwerk, and Tangerine Dream were just some of the experimenters.

Meanwhile, keyboards from the 1960s and early 1970s didn't disappear; a classic 70s keyboard line-up might have included a Hammond or other organ, piano, Rhodes, Clavinet, a Mellotron (a tape-based instrument that played back real orchestral sounds), as well as a Moog synthesizer or two.

In the early 1970s, three instruments radically simplified the process of synthesizing sound, making it a practical possibility for the working musician. The Minimoog, with its limited but flexible control panel, led the way in accessibility; the ARP 2600 featured a hard-wired setup that could be over-ridden with patch-cords; and EMS settled on a pin matrix system for the Synthi AKS, its entry into the commercial market. A system began to emerge for organizing the building blocks of synthesis into a transportable unit. That basic organizational framework has survived the ups and downs of the music technology market, the arrival of software synths, and the development of virtual analog systems. It survives because the elements are easy enough to understand, but flexible enough to be interesting and inspiring.

At the most basic level, you need an oscillator to initiate the noise, a filter to change its timbre, and an amplifier, coupled with an envelope generator and a keyboard, to say when the noise starts and how long it lasts. In the designs of the 1970s, the flow of audio signal from one element to the next would follow the path shown in the diagram to the right.

Looking from left to right, the term VCO refers to a Voltage Controlled Oscillator. That "Voltage Controlled" means that the frequency and character of the oscillator's output is determined by control voltages from elsewhere in the synthesizer: from the keyboard, the control panel, or another oscillator. In the diagram, as in a Minimoog, there are two VCOs plus one LFO, a Low Frequency Oscillator. The LFO can be used for making noises, but is more likely to be used to transform other parameters.

For each oscillator there is a choice of waveform; common options include sine waves, square waves, sawtooth, and pulse waveforms. Each waveform has its own sonic characteristic; some are richer in overtones or upper harmonics, some are smoother. The sine wave is closest to an uncolored fundamental tone; its sound can be compared to a softly blown flute. The square and sawtooth waves contain harmonics that add upper color to the sound. The square wave generates odd harmonics only—the third, fifth, and so on—which translates into a hollow, reedy quality. The sawtooth is the richest sound, as it contains an even spread of harmonics; it can be equated with a brass sound. The pulse waveform is useful for imitating string sounds.

The audio signal from the oscillators is combined in the mixer, before being routed to the next stage. Sometimes there's an option of adding white noise into the mix. It contains all frequencies at an equal level, and is very good for roughing up the sound or for *Star Wars* effects.

The next stage is the VCF (Voltage Controlled Filter), which tends to come in two types: low-pass and high-pass. The most common is the lowpass filter. It lets through all the frequencies when fully open, but progressively blocks the higher frequencies as it is closed down. If you were to play a high note on the keyboard, setting the VCF to "off" would probably extinguish the fundamental as well as the upper tones, resulting in silence. Mostly though, the VCF is used to make fine adjustments to the presence of upper harmonics: that is, how much top/brightness there is to the sound. In that way a detailed, bright string patch can become a smooth distant pad at the turn of a knob. Not surprising then, that every self-respecting synth has a way of grabbing this parameter easily and quickly.

As part of the filter section, the resonance control, also

known as "Q" or filter emphasis, plays a part in shaping the sound. Used in subtle ways, the resonance control emphasizes frequencies either side of the frequency to which its cutoff control is set, in the same way that the resonant box of an instrument such as the violin accentuates the frequencies of the strings. Used in more extreme ways, the filter squeaks and bleeps, and clicks arise when the resonance is set so high that the filter starts to self-oscillate. If it is set right you can even play these sounds as a pitch.

The final stage, the VCA (Voltage Controlled Amplifier) not only dictates the final audio level, it determines what happens when a key is pressed, held down, and released. Its envelope generator shapes the sound in time. ADSR stands for the parameters you can adjust in the envelope generator: Attack, Decay, Sustain, and Release. Attack controls how long it takes for the sound to reach its full level when the key is pressed. Decay controls how long it takes for the sound to drop to the Sustain level. Sustain is the level the sound maintains until the key is released. Release determines how long the sound continues once the key is released. Early synthesizers did not always allow the adjustment of all the parameters of the sound envelope: some just had ADS or ADR envelopes. A second envelope generator was also common.

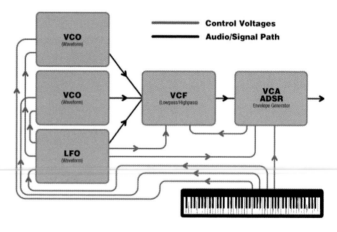

The LFO can produce sounds, as we have seen, but it has another use. It can be patched to another oscillator to "modulate" its output. In other words, it supplies an oscillating control voltage that can alter the pitch of one of the VCOs. If the LFO's waveform is set to a sine wave, it will make the VCO's pitch move gently up and down, producing vibrato. If it is set to sawtooth, the pitch will rise gently and drop rapidly, producing a harsher "nee-naw" effect. You can also use the LFO's oscillating voltage to control the cutoff of a filter, making the timbre of the sound change. And if you apply the LFO's voltage to the VCA you can have a tremolo effect.

The possibilities of an analog setup are endless—or "limited only by your imagination," as the manufacturers say—because the routing of the component modules to one another can be very complex indeed. You can apply an envelope to a filter or the waveform of an oscillator; you can use the velocity of the keyboard to control a filter's cutoff; and so on. Combining hard-wired circuits with patch-cord modulation applied to multiple destinations can cause havoc—creative havoc—to an oscillator trying to behave in a stable manner.

Thanks to Bob Moog, Alan Pearlman at ARP, and David Cockerell at EMS, the synthesizer became a player's instrument, rather than an educational programmer's tool.

Now imagine a world without VCOs, where instead of having oscillators as your starting point, your building blocks are audio recordings, digitally preserved in the memory of your keyboard. That's roughly where we are today; from home low-end keyboards to high-end synthesizer workstations, the sound is sourced from ROM wave memory. This means that instead of "synthesizing" a guitar sound, what you are doing is playing back a recording of a guitar, in exactly the same way as a sampler does. The usual filter and envelope controls are still available, and if you want to synthesize from scratch, most synths include a chunk of the basic saw, sine, square, and so on in their waveform list. However, if you want to truly synthesize in the digital age, you'll have to look for a physical modeling structure, where the synth/computer actually mimics the behavior of an analog circuit, or blown pipe, or bowed string. That's a whole other ball game.

SYNTH LEAD CD53

Sometimes it is easier to get a wild and wacky sound from an early synth than it is a conventional melody. Early synths were monophonic, meaning you could only play one note at a time. And all the parameters had to be set on the front panel, with no means of storing your sounds. Going from sensitive ballad to full-on rocking required either extensive knob-twiddling or turning to another pre-prepared Minimoog.

Calling up a lead synth patch on a modern keyboard is much easier than programming it from scratch. The choices will be between a flute-like whistle, a raucous "synch," or a brassy "phatt" sound. This last patch, probably labelled "Mini" of some sort, is the one to choose: Moog synths, which this patch imitates, have always been known for their roundness of timbre and the speed of response of the envelopes.

Check the CD at this point. This single-line exercise is modeled on Ike and Tina Turner's 1973 hit "Nutbush City Limits," an urgent rhythm track with a synth solo soaring over the top. You'll notice the sound is reluctant to move from note to note; that's because "glide" or "portamento" is engaged. The higher the setting of "glide," the longer the time to travel to the next pitch. Overdo it and the whole thing turns into a pitch-less drifting mess. Try it, then turn back the glide control for a more usable and musical effect. The instruction "pitch mod" is an invitation to turn your synth's modulation wheel, which is most likely pre-programmed to introduce a vibrato effect.

Example 5.1, "Nutmeg City"

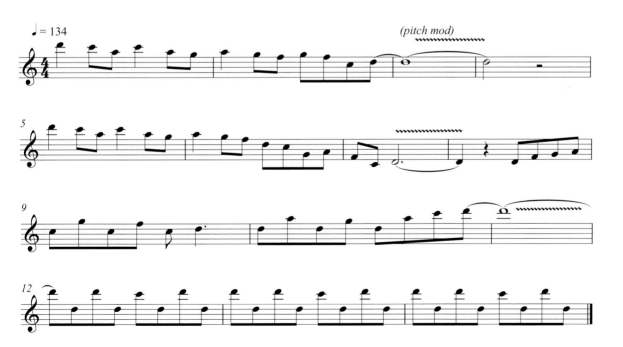

Here are three snippets, included more for their interest than as a practical playing exercise. Each refers to an iconic moment from the early 1970s, and each involves musicians forward-thinking enough to be fascinated by the world of synthesis. The first two instances are centred on the EMS synths, the VCS3 (aka the Putney) and the Synthi AKS. Both had the same synth circuitry, but the AKS had a sequencer on board, perfect for a looping around of eight notes.

Pink Floyd had one at their disposal during the sessions for *The Dark Side Of The Moon*; for the tune "On The Run," they sequenced up something like the pattern in 5.2a. Set it running, speed it up, play with the cutoff frequency to change the timbre, and you have instant chase music. The riff can be played with the left hand, so call up a fast synth patch, access the cutoff parameter and twiddle away, remembering to start slowly and build up speed.

Snippet 5.2b, uses the VCS3, the AKS's precursor, to play

what is essentially a synth feature rather than a solo. Roxy Music's "Virginia Plain" is the inspiration, with Bryan Ferry on piano and Brian Eno on synth. Two hands are required for this one. Take the middle of the Cs with the left hand to start with. After a few times round, switch to right hand to see how it feels.

Snippet 5.2c, is probably unplayable, but that's the point. Machines can play things fingers can't, so it's good to learn how to tell the machines to play the unplayable. We will return to sequencing in Unit Six, but for now, play or enter these notes into your sequencer of choice. The bewildering thing is the 16th-note triplets in the bottom part against the 16th-notes of the upper. The track that inspired this riff is "Baba O'Riley," from *Who's Next*. You can tell where Pete Townshend's head was at: the "Baba" was guru Meher Baba, whose ideas were coursing around at the time, while O'Riley was Terry Riley, the "systems" music composer.

Examples 5.2a, 5.2b, and 5.3c, "Run Don't Walk," "Dear Virginia", and "Terry O'Meher"

The Moog entered Stevie Wonder's life in quite a big way. In 1971 he heard a record called Zero Time, by TONTO's Expanding Head Band, otherwise known as Robert Margouleff and Malcolm Cecil. It used an assemblage of synths by Oberheim, ARP, and EMS, all in orbit around a Series III Moog modular set-up. The sonic potential of these instruments bowled Wonder over, so he hired Cecil and Margouleff (and TONTO, which stood for The Original New Timbral Orchestra) and produced his awesome early-70s albums. TONTO was used for lead-lines, for semi-orchestral mock-ups, and for basslines. This piece is modeled on "Boogie On Reggae Woman," from the 1974 album *Fulfillingness' First Finale*.

The first thing to notice about this piece is that although you would expect a bass part to be taken by the left hand, the technical agility and wheel manipulation involved dictate use of the right hand. To the left of most keyboards are two revolving wheels. The left one is routinely assigned to varying the pitch of the note up or down by a tone, while the right is conventionally assigned to introducing a pitch variation sounding like a wobbly vibrato. The use of both of these is central to "humanizing" the otherwise inexpressive sound of early synths. Having tried the modulation wheel, it's time to get familiar with pitch bend. Imagine you're bending a string in the manner of a guitarist, stretching the top note of the phrase and letting it fall again. Some bend wheels are sprung to return to a central position, while others have an indentation so that you can feel where zero is.

Example 5.3, "Boogie Along"

Let's leave synthesizers for a while and look at what else was going on in the 1960s and 70s. Of all the instruments to emerge during that time, the Fender Rhodes has held the most consistent interest—particularly in the jazz world—since the moment Miles Davis sat a slightly reluctant Keith Jarrett down in front of one.

Miles was making some of the most vital music of the time; albums such as *In A Silent Way*, *Bitches Brew*, and *A Tribute To Jack Johnson* changed jazz in the same way Dylan had changed folk. The keyboard players he was working with back then would leave deep footprints. Keith Jarrett became one of the world's finest improvisers; Herbie Hancock became one of the freest, most free-wheeling musicians ever to grace a platform; Chick Corea joined the elite of jazz composers and players; and Joe Zawinul was a true original.

Hancock's album *Head Hunters* made a big splash in 1973, and it is the Rhodes style that distinguishes it, as well as the use of Clavinet (which we'll come to later) and other more exotic

keyboards. On this page is "Chrysalis," a brief glimpse into the jazz/fusion world of Hancock's 1970s bands. In one sense tonal life is fairly straightforward. An F7 serves to cover the first eight bars, except for the chromatic rise at the start.

This stability is a result of the funk content. But what is trickier is what's put on top of that basic chord. Additions, or extensions, abound in the form of sharpened ninths, flattened fifths, and suspended fourths. Bar eight contains the classic Hancock tremolo: not an electric effect this time but a right-hand oscillation between two notes of an octave that is the "percussive" keyboard player's way of creating "sustain." The 11th chords are typical of Hancock: they stack up through seventh and ninth to 11, which is a fourth an octave up. Leave out the third to avoid a fourth/third clash. The Bb11 in bar ten is the full voicing.

To play this piece use a classic Rhodes sound or sample as opposed to a synthesizer emulation of an electric piano. The Rhodes is on the left channel on the CD.

Example 5.4, "Chrysalis"

"Chrysalis Two" expands the previous piece with a Clavinet part designed to mesh with the Rhodes. The gaps are long, particularly in the second bar of each pair. The hardest note to time is the final offbeat 16th-note in bar one. Choose your finest clav sound, perhaps with auto-wah, and keep every note as short as possible until the change of mood at bar nine. The chords following bar nine are a string of 11th chords, basically. This is a sound that Hancock used very effectively. His "Maiden Voyage" uses them to migrate between relatively unrelated keys: a Dm11 is followed by an Fm11 then an E♭11 and so on. Because the sound of the chord is so stable, it can be shunted around the keys with relative ease.

Enharmonic key changes (where the sound stays the same but the way it is written changes) are a problem; at bar 11 the

G♭maj7 is followed by an E/F♯ slash chord. This is a bit of a jolt to the brain, to be so suddenly shifted from one world of accidentals to another. But thealternative is to re-label the second chord F♭/G♭, which no-one wants to look at, let alone work out, or to re-label the first chord F♯maj7, which is a jolt considering that the previous two bars use "flat" chords. Sense and ease of reading dictate here, but bear in mind that there are always other options.

The chords in the F section are included just in case you fancy taking a solo on top of the clav part with the right hand. This means memorizing the left hand or keeping the right hand sparse where there is action in the bass—or possibly both. Pay attention to the alterations of the F7 chord; where you would use the Mixolydian, try a wholetone scale, which is illustrated in the tune.

Example 5.5, "Chrysalis Two"

PENTATONIC SCALES

World music with improvisation has been around since the 1970s, and arguably before that if you consider the worldwide popularity of Brazil's bossa nova movement. The group that took it to new heights, and flung the doors open to all world styles, was Weather Report, led by saxophonist Wayne Shorter and keyboardist Joe Zawinul. Zawinul not only showed it was possible to display a strong sense of musical identity using synths, he also wrote some of the strongest tunes of the late 20th century.

One of Zawinul's trademark synth basslines, the intro to "Birdland," has become legendary, and his soloing style, often using pentatonic scale patterns, was mesmerizing. If you want to emulate him, speed of execution is vital: the "blurred" effect, coupled with slips into other tonal areas and back, is at first dazzling.

The pentatonic (five notes per octave) scale, used widely in ethnic music, is an ideal improvising tool as nothing can sound wrong; any note you play will work, which is quite a relief. The pentatonic scale crops up in Native American, Chinese, Japanese, and Celtic musics—everywhere, really—in two main forms, the major (C) pentatonic, and the minor (A) pentatonic. As you can see, the notes are the same, it just depends on your starting point. "Penta" is a simple pentatonic exercise. After reading and playing it, try it in groups of five (five fingers, five notes) and expand the exercise upward. The possibilities are vast.

Example 5.6, "Penta"

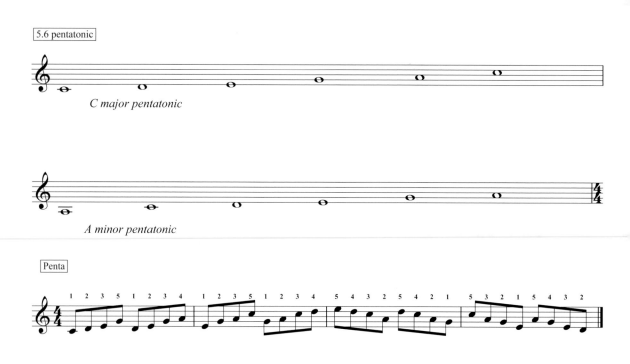

5.6 pentatonic

C major pentatonic

A minor pentatonic

Penta

"Market A.M." is based on the G pentatonic, as if played by Zawinul on a reedy solo synth with plenty of pitch bend and modulation; so, left hand on the wheels, if you have them.

It could be that you have a joystick, where side movement controls pitch and upward vertical movement engages modulation. Downward vertical is sometimes used for filter modulation, which means either manually opening or closing the filter, or doing it automatically in the same way as a vibrato or tremolo is introduced by a low frequency oscillator (LFO). Some keyboard controllers give you a choice between joystick and wheels; most keyboards plump for one or the other. An additional ribbon controller, a plastic flat strip four inches long, is increasingly included on modern keyboards; it's a very intuitive

device for sliding pitch or controlling filter cutoff. It is easy to get carried away with modulation wheels and controllers, though. Always use them with discretion; excessive use can lead to listener annoyance.

'Market P.M.' is a similar idea to "Market A.M." but it includes more 16th-note passages, "blue" notes, and the "outside of the harmony" areas that Zawinul was often keen to explore. In this case the B-flat is the blues third, and the B-flat and the E-flat in succession suggest a superimposed harmony of E-flat, which is a distant cousin of the home key, G major. Try other triads over the pedal G—a D-flat for instance—that introduces a flattened fifth and seventh as against the existing major seventh. The last two notes of bar two hint at this.

Example 5.7a, "Market A.M."

Example 5.7b, "Market P.M."

Although they don't inhabit the same musical area, Chick Corea and Joe Sample are two players who share a directness of line when soloing and an understanding of the paring-down involved when playing any electric piano, particularly the Rhodes. Sample's work with The Crusaders is testament to his love of the Rhodes sound, and Corea's albums *Light As A Feather* and *Friends* illustrate perfectly the art of distilling the fistfuls of notes that one might play on acoustic piano to mere handfuls. The left-hand voicings in "Joe's Friends" contain a maximum of three notes, quite often bunched together and including a whole step/half-step crunch.

Placement of these crunches against the rhythm is central to the piece, which has a Latin flavor. Corea, in particular was quick to absorb sounds from South America and the Caribbean,

in particular Afro-Cuban and Brazilian styles. *Light As A Feather* emphasises the Brazilian, being almost a showcase for percussionist Airto Moreira, whom Corea had met working on *Bitches Brew*. The Brazilian rhythm in "Joe's Friends" is a samba, and the accents of the groove are written in the bass clef of bars one and two. Tap the pattern to get it under the skin, in the right hand and left hand separately. Next get the left-hand chords sounding right, then check the CD for a mechanistic approximation of the sinuous, lithe, slinky, vivacious thing that is a samba groove. Corea's left-hand crispness is exemplary at all times, the staccato leaving plenty of air and skip in the track. Latin music is often written in "cut time," as here, half-notes being the main pulse rather than the fast quarter-notes.

Example 5.8, "Joe's Friends"

You couldn't find two players at more opposite ends of the keyboard spectrum than Chick Corea and Richard Wright. Wright has been responsible for keys with Pink Floyd since their inception. It's interesting to listen to *The Piper At The Gates Of Dawn*, Floyd's album from 1967, because the keyboards seem to have more contributing solo space than on the later albums, where the parts become more textural.

The sound picture is individual, too. The Farfisa organ is the main solo voice. A dual-manual combo organ, it was fed into a Binson Echorec, a delay machine, to increase the sound possibilities. "Doctor Floyd" is based on several Floyd tracks, the descending chromatic chords of the first three bars a trademark sequence. Although the content is straight down the line, with lots of flattened thirds and flattened fifths over a major/minor open tonality, what Wright does really well is shape his solos, as do all the band. There's a well crafted up-and-down shape to the register of many solos, and this one is no exception. The dotted feel is nicely idiosyncratic also.

Wright used a Hammond C-3 model with a Leslie 122 in the 1970s and later. The Mellotron featured in his setup as early as 1968. It was used to sculpt semi-orchestral backdrops, as was his ARP Solina. The Minimoog is the brassy lead sound on "Shine On You Crazy Diamond," the band's homage to Syd Barrett, the brilliant but troubled guitarist on *The Piper At The Gates Of Dawn*.

Example 5.9, "Doctor Floyd"

The majority of keyboard players with the "progressive" rock bands in England at the close of the 60s and through the 1970s had experienced some degree of classical training. Jon Lord of Deep Purple, Rick Wakeman of Yes, Keith Emerson of The Nice and ELP, and Tony Banks of Genesis were were all acquainted with classical styles. This showed itself not only in their compositions, but in the way they handled accompanying passages. One technique stands out as being the texture of choice, the broken or arpeggiated chord.

From Bach's first C major prelude, from *The Well Tempered Klavier*, through Beethoven's "Moonlight" sonata, the arpeggio has a solid reputation for adding movement to slowly moving chordal progressions. Speed of movement depends on context and required effect, but this example uses 16th-notes to animate a sequence of descending chords that are redolent of classical harmony.

The right hand is the focal point, but try sustaining chords in the left hand. These can be triadic, typically using a Mellotron-ish string or choir sound, while the arpeggio patterns ripple out with a piano sound.

Example 5.10, "Showtime"

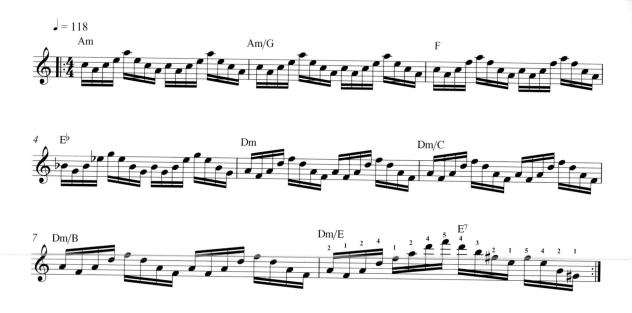

This example expands on the previous page by alternating arpeggio and scale patterns so that the resulting line draws more attention to itself, in the manner of a solo. Indeed, many a solo has been based entirely on these materials, with little rhythmic variation but a high degree of instrumental skill. Instead of the piano try a rip-roaring Moog-style lead-synth sound in the right hand.

One way to turn this into a fully fledged solo is to play the first bar as written, then improvise the second, play the third bar, and so on. After a few tries you'll be wanting to improvise through the odd as well as the even bars. Remember, though, that the golden rule in "prog" rock is to display virtuosity at

every opportunity. Why play eighth-notes when 16th-notes have so much more flair—or should that be flare?

The left hand is given some work to do here. It's very good for your independence to be able to arpeggiate a self-accompaniment in the left while being busy with the right. Try a piano sound in your left hand; or continue with the strings/choral approach of the previous page if the sound "speaks" quickly enough to make the arpeggios work.

If the whole thing sounds like a piece of 18th-century baroque, don't panic. Just wait till the guitar, bass, and drums drop by.

Example 5.11, "Showtime Solo"

It's 1975 and the sound of disco is beginning to ripple across the States. *Saturday Night Fever* is still two years away, but The Bee Gees are in search of a new direction. Producer Arif Mardin suggests soul and rhythm & blues would be a good direction to take, and "Jive Talkin'" is the result. Almost the first thing you hear is a bass synth, burbling far too low in its register to make musical sense, along with a scratchy guitar. But let's focus on the synth.

From "Boogie On Reggae Woman" to Donna Summer's "State Of Independence," the bassline synth has a real cut to its timbre. It's an initial splurge of upper harmonics, which are then shut out as the note continues in a sort of "baaoooonng" noise. What's happening in synth terms is that the filter is open on the front end of every note, and gradually closes a moment later. This is achieved by modulating the filter with a second envelope generator, the first being still in use to control the overall shape of the sound. If the levels of attack, sustain, and release on the second envelope generator are set to zero, then the D (decay) time will open and close the filter. The shorter the time, the more abrupt the "ba …"

Try this: select a bass sound close to that on the CD, probe around in the edit menu of your synth for the filter parameters, then locate the filter modifier: it might be called Envelope 2. Vary the amount and compare the effect.

Having refined your sound, turn to "Hand Jive" and play bass with the CD. The solo drum track is provided (CD track 63) so you can play bass and Rhodes together. This entails playing the bass with your left hand, which is very good practice indeed.

Example 5.12, "Hand Jive"

Continuing in the disco vein, let's turn to another great producer, Giorgio Moroder, and his partnership with singer Donna Summer. In 1977, with "I Feel Love," they virtually invented a style that would transform music right through to techno and electronica.

The machines have arrived; which is why it's really worth having a go at "Play, Don't Feel." The top line of the page, 5.13a, is an exact transcription of the bassline on the CD, but it is unplayable by human hand to any great degree of accuracy. Move alternate notes up an octave however and you have a much more playable left-hand right-hand double-act, moved out of each other's way: 5.13b.

That is OK as far as it goes, but what if you were to set up a split, or use a second keyboard, with the top sound lowered by an octave? Then what you play would be 5.13b, and what you hear would be 5.13a. To carry the process to the limit, pan the two keyboard areas left and right and there you have it, a performable disco bassline.

The clavinet part is added for accuracy rather than playability: you're in enough trouble already.

"Play Don't Feel" moves the riff up the minor thirds of a diminished chord. This is a useful compositional device, because you end up back where you started, on the D. Repeat this tune round (without the CD) until you can't stand any more.

Example 5.13, "Play, Don't Feel"

As a complete antidote to the previous piece, relax with the slowly moving chords of "Strange Dreams," a track that owes something to a Tangerine Dream tune, "Mysterious Semblance At The Strand Of Nightmares," from their 1974 album, *Phaedra*, where the synths are awash with resonating filter sweeps.

Try "Strange Dreams" on just one synth pad, but make absolutely sure you can access the cutoff and resonance parameters of your filter section. Use the sustain pedal to hold

chords, and whizz and fizz through the chord changes, using those cutoff and resonance controls to shape the harmonics. At some point make sure you turn up the resonance control enough to make the filter itself oscillate. But take care you don't do it too violently or you will destroy the mood with synth shrieks. As a synthesizer/keyboard player, you should know at what setting your board starts to squeal; each one is slightly different.

The metronome marking is for real, by the way.

Example 5.14, "Strange Dreams"

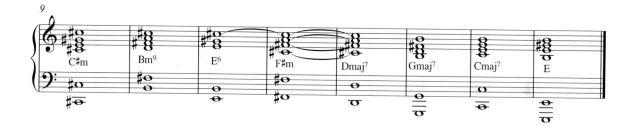

Orchestras of synthesizers had their beginnings with Walter/Wendy Carlos's score for Stanley Kubrick's *A Clockwork Orange*, which was a collection of original and classical pieces played on a modular instrument. TONTO, Cecil and Margouleff's baby, was another such recording device, while the electronic music studios in the States and Europe all had serious systems. But a band playing synthesizer music live?

Then, in 1976, Jean-Michel Jarre created his groundbreaking album *Oxygène*. Jarre had studied experimental electronic music in Paris with Pierre Schaeffer,

the pioneer of *musique concrète*, but his album had a strong and accessible melodic sound that made it a huge commercial success when it was released internationally in 1977. He went on to give concerts that broke all attendance records.

Meanwhile, in Germany, two synthesizer bands had emerged: Kraftwerk and Tangerine Dream. Tangerine Dream were formed in 1967 by Edgar Froese, who was joined by Christopher Franke and Peter Baumann in a three-keyboard line-up for the band's most influential mid-1970s period.

The other German synth band, Kraftwerk, grew out of the avant-garde electronic music scene of the late 1960s. The group was founded by keyboardist Ralf Hütter and Florian Schneider, who played flute, violin, and synthesizer. By the the tour for the group's breakthrough album, *Autobahn*, Kraftwerk had become a quartet, with Wolfgang Flür and Karl Bartos on electronic percussion.

Kraftwerk's music seems to show a lack of feeling and involvement until you realize that you've been drawn in by the slightest emotional trigger. The percussion element set them apart, giving them a cleaner sound than Tangerine Dream. It was a sound that has never gone away, the semi-robotic sequencing having become a constant element in subsequent forms of dance music.

"Quarter Past Five" has quite a few staves, because both bass and the accompanying "synth 2" line are notated. These patterns carry on to bar 10, before chords make their presence felt. The two synth melodies, meanwhile, chase each other before coming together at the same point. To get the feel of each line, run it through with the percussion track on the CD (track 67), then play the two synth melodies with the full version (track 66).

White noise is often the origin of synthesized percussion. It's a relatively easy task to set up a patch: white noise goes to filter, filter to ADSR, Envelope 2 modulates the filter. Careful adjustment of decay and release, and refinement at the filter stage, provide convincing results.

Example 5.15, "Quarter Past Five"

The 1980s were years of extraordinary development in the keyboard world, with the advent of digital synthesis, drum machines, MIDI, sequencing, and sampling. All this innovation came with a hefty price tag: Fairlight's original Computer Musical Instrument system, introduced in 1979, would have set you back a whopping $25,000.

Progress was rapid, however, and by 1981 E-MU Systems had brought out the first affordable keyboard-based sampler, the Emulator. Then, in 1983, MIDI (Musical Instrument Digital Interface) was introduced. For the first time it allowed electronic musical instruments, computers, and other equipment to communicate and synchronize with each other.

These developments opened the door for synthesizer-based music, which had its roots in the pioneering work of Kraftwerk, Yellow Magic Orchestra, Jean-Michel Jarre, and Ultravox. Groups like Duran Duran and Depeche Mode now created a more commercial form of synth-based music, referred to as synthpop, and the charts were dominated by it, with hits by Gary Numan, Soft Cell, Eurythmics, and The Human League. The Art Of Noise, with producer Trevor Horn, pioneered sample-based music, making extensive use of the Fairlight CMI.

In the United States a new music emerged from Michigan. The Detroit techno sound merged European synth-pop with funk and soul to create a new type of dance music. It made particular use of the Roland TR303 and TR808 drum machines and analog synths.

Detroit techno was particularly influenced by the electronic disco music of Italian-born producer Giorgio Moroder, who created huge international hits for Donna Summer ("I Feel Love," 1977) and Irene Cara ("Flashdance," 1983). See Unit Five for more on Moroder and Summer.

Sequencing and sampling became integral to creating music in the 80s, and some musicians feared for their jobs. However, as with all new technologies, musicians, and especially keyboard players, had to adapt. They did so by becoming programmers and arrangers.

With the introduction of the "workstation," a digital sampling keyboard with a built-in sequencer, it became possible for anyone to produce decent quality music at home, leading to the "bedroom studio" phenomenon. Eventually the computer would replace the workstation, for most people, as computer-based sequencing software like Cubase and Logic became available. It had far more advanced editing capabilities, and took full advantage of the increasing processing power of the new computers.

These groundbreaking years have informed the way music is produced today and left a legacy of great music. In this unit we will look at the major styles to emerge from this decade and put the synthesizer through its paces. We will focus on the different roles that the synthesizer can play, including producing synthetic sounds, emulating real instruments, and combining the two to create new and exciting sounds.

ANALOG SOUNDS

Although analog synthesizers can be used to re-produce real sounds, they are best at creating "synth sounds'. Some of the greatest hits of the 80s owe their success to these instruments—and their talented composers, of course. The opening figure of Soft Cell's "Tainted Love" and the bassline to The Eurhythmics' "Sweet Dreams" are classic synth parts.

The basis of any synth sound is the waveform that is used to create it. As explained in the Keyboard Facts book, synthesizers use voltage controlled oscillator (VCOs) to generate waveforms. The diagram explains how these look and sound. Each waveform has a unique set of harmonics (overtones), which color the sound.

Keyboard Splits

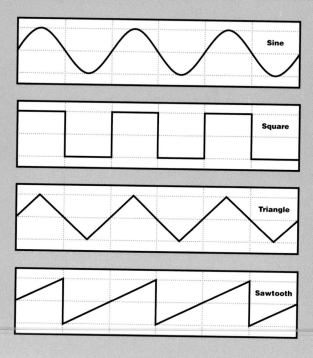

The sine wave has a very pure sound and is used to create solo synth sounds and a smooth bass sound.

The square wave has a mellow sound similar to that of a clarinet.

The triangle wave is similar to that made by a violin string when bowed.

The sawtooth wave produces a bright sound and is a good starting point for brassy sounds.

SAWTOOTH WAVE

CD68

Two analog synths that emerged at the beginning of the 1980s were the Roland Juno 6 and the Korg Polysix. Both had six-note polyphony, meaning that six notes could be played simultaneously. Analog synths are capable of producing some very fat sounds, due to their multiple oscillators and chorus/phasing type effects.

"Pretty Poly" uses a sound derived from a sawtooth waveform. The newer digital instruments and software synths are able to reproduce analog sounds, so if you're using one of these you want to look for a sound labeled "poly-synth" or something similar. This type of sound is good for both single lines and chordal parts and can be heard on Van Halen's "Jump"

and Deniece Williams' "Let's Hear It For The Boy."

In this piece, the right hand uses triads against a quarter-note bassline. It's important to keep the left hand as steady as possible so that the right-hand syncopations are effective. This type of bass part can be used to beef up an existing bassline or even replace it all together.

A couple of easy adjustments can be made to alter the sound. In the editing section of your synth, locate the filter page. Adjusting the cut-off point of the filter up or down will alter the sound's tonal quality. Experiment with this to get the tone you want. You can also make the sound appear "wider" by adding a chorus effect.

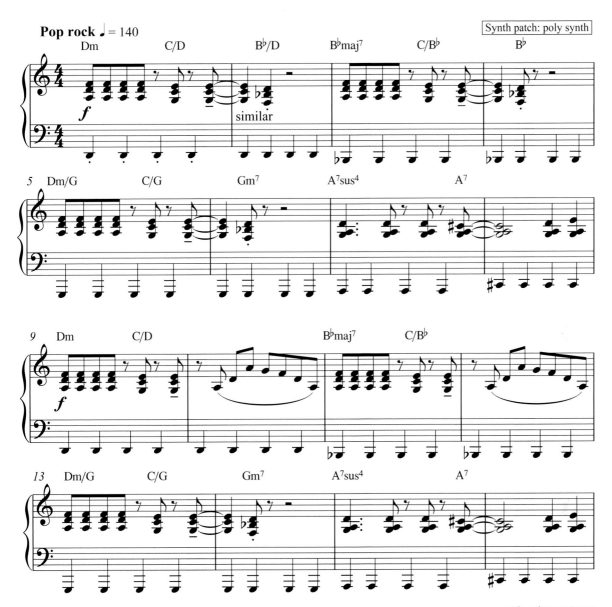

continued on next page

Bands like Depeche Mode, Yazoo, and OMD built up their tracks using multiple keyboard parts. These break down into several categories including basslines, rhythmic chordal parts, sustained chords, and melodic lines.

If we take a sound created from a square wave we get quite a hollow tone, similar to that of a clarinet. It is bright and able to cut through. This type of sound is good for single-line repetitive parts and can be used for an instrumental interlude or a backing figure around a vocal line.

Listen to the CD to hear the sound. See if you can find something similar on your keyboard.

In "Small Town Girl" the notes should be played short and spiky. Try adjusting the attack and the release of the sound. This can be done by locating the ADSR (Attack-Decay-Sustain-Release) controls in the edit section of your synth. (See Unit 5 for more information.) Increasing or decreasing the attack will cause the sound to have a softer or harsher front edge. If you adjust the release parameter, the sound will become shorter or longer. All four of the parameters work together, so experiment a little to see what you can create.

The single-line melody is built around the chord tones, with some passing scale notes. Although the part is repetitive there is some simple variation, which keeps it interesting. Try to create your own single-line part using the chord sequence as a basis.

Example 6.2, "Small Town Girl"

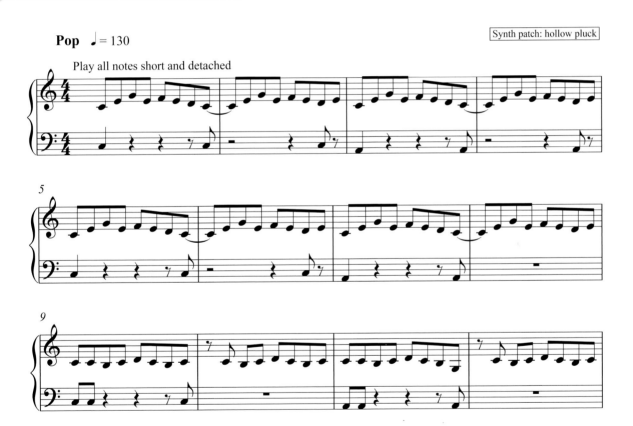

continued on next page

TRIANGLE WAVE

Synths are great at filling in space on a track by creating a wash of sound. This is called a "pad." Pads are used to provide harmony and create atmosphere; they usually have a mellow sound with a slow attack. It is best to play chordal, sustained parts, usually in whole or half-notes.

The sound for "The Apartment" is created from a triangle wave. Once again, listen to the track and find a similar sound on your keyboard. No surprises here; we are just playing chords. However, to keep the part interesting it's good to play around with the inversions and the octaves in which you place the chords.

In reality you wouldn't change around so often; you might reserve an octave change for the last chorus in a song, or play a different inversion on the second verse.

Example 6.3, "The Apartment"

DISCO

Disco is a form of dance music with its origins in soul and funk. It started in the 1970s and was made popular by acts like Donna Summer and The Village People. The groove consists of a four-on-the-floor bass drum pattern with hi-hats on eighth-notes and 16th-notes. (This will be covered in greater detail in Unit Seven.) Against that there is often a syncopated bassline, electric piano, string, and horn lines.

Strings are one of the sounds that can be reproduced quite convincingly by digital keyboards. Most keyboards have several choices of string patch.

Choose a string patch with a hard attack because "Disco Strings," which follows, played at a fast tempo. Make sure it's a multi-string patch and not a solo instrument like violin or viola: this will give you a full range of sound across the keyboard.

As string parts usually contain fast patterns or runs we need to do some preliminary exercises to get ready for the piece.

Example 6.4, Pentatonic Exercises

C minor pentatonic

Four-note pattern

Three-note pattern

"Disco Strings" includes many of the techniques you'll need to know when copying or creating your own string parts. In bars one and five there is a small line after each of the quarter-notes. This is a short glissando or "gliss." As string players create notes by placing their fingers on the strings they can also slip up to or away from the notes. To recreate this effect on the keyboard use the pitch-bend wheel. You only want to change the pitch by a small amount, so check to see what your keyboard's pitch-bend setting is and change it to two half-steps (or semitones).

In the bridge section the eighth-note phrases are marked with a slur, so be sure to play them legato (smoothly). The chorus uses long sustained phrases that outline the chords. This is very typical in string parts. Watch out for the scales in bars 21 and 33; with the correct fingering you should be able to play them. Also pay special attention to the articulation (accents, staccato, etc) and dynamics.

There are two ways of achieving the dynamics marked throughout the part; either use the volume fader, which is fine as long as you are not using your left hand, or better still, attach a volume pedal to your keyboard.

Note that the second chorus is a repeat of the first except an octave higher; this is a simple but effective way of creating variation and excitement.

Example 6.5, "Disco Strings"

continued on next page

"Disco Strings Two" is a re-working of the original tune with the addition of a left-hand part to create a fuller sound. There are several ways to harmonize a string part and "Disco Strings Two" uses the most common of these.

In the verse, an octave below has been added to the left hand, which adds weight. The left hand in the bridge outlines the roots of the chord and adds some extra movement in bar seven,

ending up in a spread chord on the first beat of bar nine. The chorus melody is harmonized using thirds.

Verse two again sees some octave doubling, in bar 23, and the final chorus is doubled an octave below with bars 38 and 39 having a three-octave unison spread. When you've completed this, see if you can come up with your own harmonization and try it out with "Disco Strings."

Example 6.6, "Disco Strings Two"

continued on next page

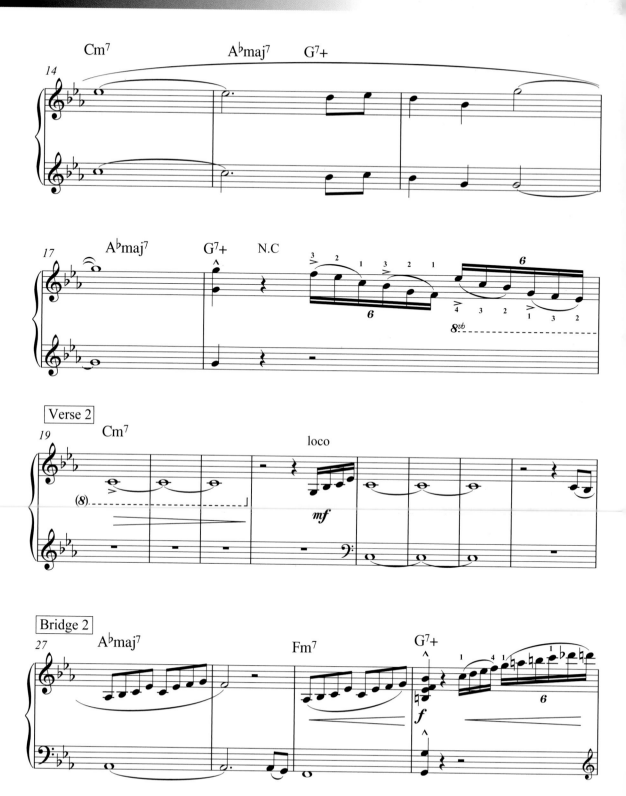

Pro tip

Many keyboards can layer sounds (play two sounds at once). So instead of having to play octave melodies with both hands, set your string patch to include the octave below. This give the illusion of two string parts at once and leaves your left hand free to play another keyboard. Also experiment with layering two different string sounds. One could be used for its fast attack, and another, warmer patch could fatten out the sound.

Keyboard players are often called upon to take the place of a brass section. As with the strings, articulation and dynamics are the key to creating a realistic sound. Modern keyboards often have sampled brass sounds that can re-produce the swells and falls that are intrinsic to brass players, but with older-style keyboards we need to use the volume pedal and pitchwheel respectively. Choose a bright brass sound for this piece; we need plenty of front-end attack to make the punchy rhythmic figures stand out.

Bars 25 and 34 have a long wiggly line after them; this indicates that the note should fall. You can use the pitch-bend wheel to do this. Make sure the pitch-bend parameter is set at around seven (half-steps) and be sure to let go of the note before you release the pitch wheel. Alternatively, you can play a short gliss with your thumb.

Example 6.7, "Disco Brass"

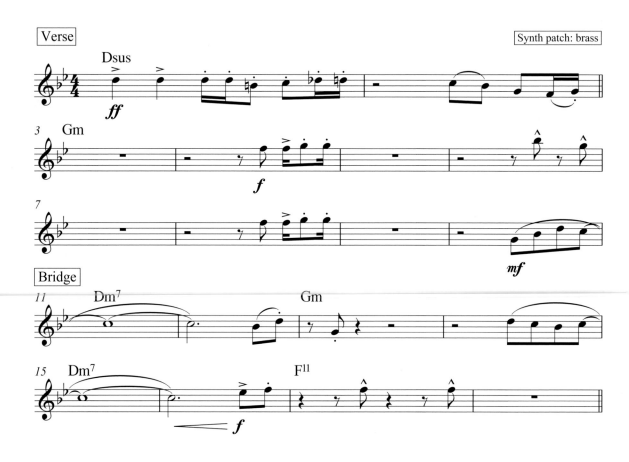

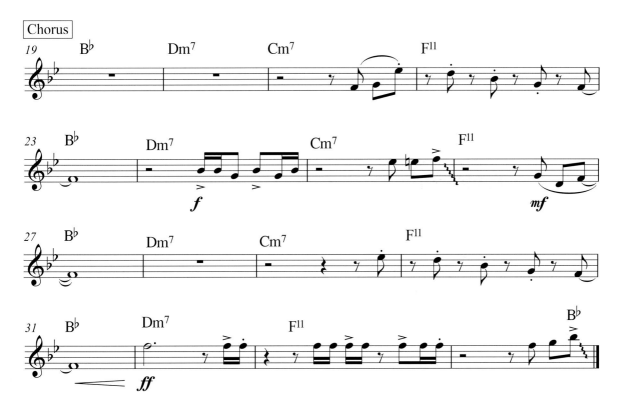

Pro tip

The term brass means a brass section. This usually consists of trumpets, saxophones, and trombones in varying shapes and sizes. In order to stay realistic, try not to play too high or too low. The average trumpet player can reach top C two octaves above middle C and the lowest note on a trombone is the E below the bass clef. Middle C is always referred to as C3 in midi terminology. There is a chart of brass ranges on the next page. Each instrument is shown at its sounding pitch.

Now we've added a left-hand part to create "Disco Brass Two." It uses some of the same techniques that we learned in "Disco Strings Two."

By adding the octave below in the verse we really beef up the part. Make sure that you play both parts strictly in time; if there's even a slight variation the part will feel weak.

The chords have been harmonized in the bridge and the chorus, which has a four-bar repeating chord sequence. Notice that there is a small variation each time. You should really be in the disco mood now, so if you want to hear some really great brass and string lines, check out Earth Wind & Fire, Barry White, and Gloria Gaynor.

Example 6.8, "Disco Brass Two"

ACOUSTIC SOUNDS

Most keyboards come programmed with several acoustic instruments: for instance, brass, guitar, harp, and oboe.

The main thing to remember is to stay within the real instrument's range. This is not a comprehensive list, but some of the most commonly found instrument ranges are included.

When playing a single line instrument, try not to overlap notes; this would be impossible to do on the real instrument.

With guitar sounds, it can be quite difficult to reproduce the strumming effect, but single-line riffs and melodies work well, as do broken chords and arpeggiated patterns.

Instrument Ranges

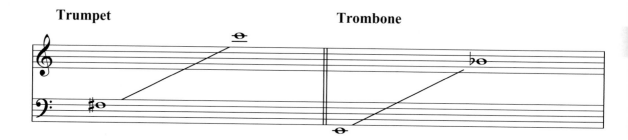

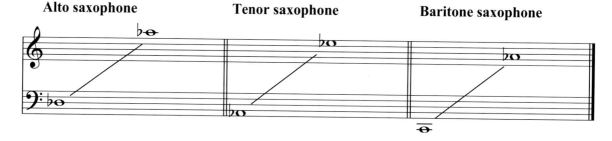

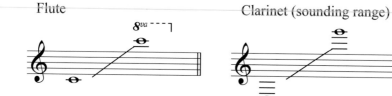

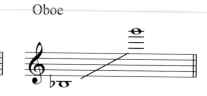

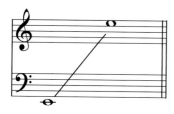

So far we've looked at analog sounds and reproducing real instruments. Digital technology opened up a new world of sound, in which samples could be mixed with synthesized waveforms and processed with effects. In the late 1980s, the most popular keyboards were the Korg M1 and Roland D50. Each keyboard had its own form of synthesis, resulting in a unique sound. Manufacturers also produced their keyboards as sound modules, so you could layer several sounds at once, using MIDI.

"Popsicle" explores several of these hybrid sounds, and lets you get to grips with playing two keyboards at once (or you could use a keyboard split: see over the page).

For the upper keyboard part you want a sound that is a mixture of sampled breathy voices and a synthetic waveform. It should have a long release time, so that even though you're playing short notes the sound will ring on. The lower keyboard part should have a bright synth sound with a front edge similar to that of a sampled harpsichord or clavinet. Listen to the CD to hear the kind of sounds you need. The co-ordination of the two parts in bars one to four is tricky, so try tapping out these two rhythms first. Both hands take turns at playing rhythmic patterns as well as outlining the chords. There are no fixed rules for which hand plays what, so you need to become ambidextrous.

Example 6.9, "Popsicle"

Here's where things get a little more complicated. We are going to use two keyboards, each with a split. Most modern keyboards are able to create keyboard splits, in which two different sounds are spread across a single keyboard and played independently. A split point can be set and each sound can be tuned up or down to get it to the pitch where you need it.

In this case, the left hand of the top keyboard is tuned up an octave so that it sounds at the pitch written in the music. To play it at the correct pitch you have to play it one octave lower than it is written. (Consult your instrument's manual to find out how to set up a keyboard split.)

The diagrams opposite show the two-keyboard setup for "Popsicle Split" with the split points for each keyboard labeled. The top keyboard is split at G4, which is the G above Middle C.

Middle C is called C4 in midi terminology; an octave below is C3 and so on. The bottom keyboard is split at A3, which is the A below Middle C. The octave transposition of the lower part of the top keyboard is marked.

In the music, the right-hand stave is played on the top keyboard and the left-hand stave is played on the bottom keyboard. The L and U indicate whether you are playing the upper or lower part of the keyboard split. One complication: in bar six the right hand moves down to the bottom keyboard to play the chord on bar six and then moves quickly back to the top keyboard.

There is a lot going on in this piece, so take your time to work out the co-ordination technicalities in bars 9–17 before trying it out with the CD.

Example 6.10, "Popsicle Split"

Keyboard Splits

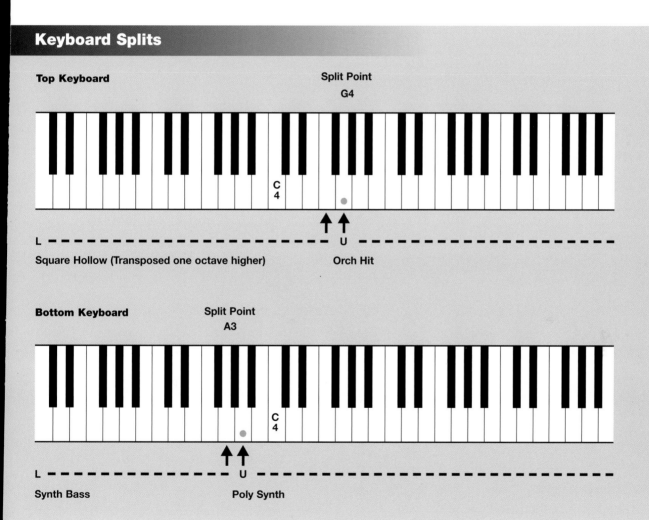

The current music scene includes such a diverse range of styles—from hip-hop and indie to alternative rock and dance and all their various sub-genres—that it would be impossible to include them all here. Instead we are going to focus on some important styles in which keyboards take a central role and explore their technical and creative requirements.

Firstly we look at the singer-songwriter genre, which has given us such greats as Joni Mitchell, Elton John, and Kate Bush as well as contemporary artists such as Alicia Keys, David Gray, Tori Amos, and Amy Winehouse. That means examining the art of piano accompaniment.

Then there are mainstream indie bands like Coldplay, Snow Patrol, and Keane, who combine guitar-based music with synthesizers to great effect. We will look at the function of the keyboard in this music and explore various sound options and combinations.

Finally we will delve into the world of dance music, with its heavy emphasis on pumping beats. Although it is primarily a producer-led genre, it has given birth to numerous successful acts, such as Basement Jaxx, Faithless, and Goldfrapp. We will look at the individual parts in detail, and the basics of sequencing, before building up a multi-layered dance track from scratch.

SINGER-SONGWRITERS

Most singer-songwriters tend to favor one of two instruments for writing, either the piano or the guitar. The piano is a versatile instrument when it comes to composing and accompaniment, because it can provide a gentle texture in a vocal ballad and add real drive to a rock song. Firstly let's take a look at what to do in a ballad.

The key thing to remember here is that the vocal is always the most important element of any song, so stay out of the way. Aim to play simply and be aware of where the melody sits, so that your chord voicings don't clash with it.

"Fortune Smiles" uses a classic piano ballad technique, where the right hand plays four chords per bar with a simple left hand bass line outlining the roots of the chords. Lionel Ritchie's 1984 hit, "Hello," uses this simple idea to great effect.

The chorus has a three-note hook and introduces a rhythmic change in bar 11. The bridge breaks up the pattern further by introducing half-notes. Although simple in themselves these rhythmic shifts help to shape the song and create interest.

Keep the right hand quarter-notes steady and even and make sure that your pedal changes are accurate.

Example 7.1, "Fortune Smiles"

Our next tune, "Fortune Accents", is a re-working of "Fortune Smiles." The basic chord shapes have been preserved but the four-in-a-bar pattern has been broken down. An element of syncopation has been introduced throughout which gives the song a more punchy feel. There is nothing too difficult here, but make sure you observe the articulation and dynamics.

Pro tip

Adding a few simple accents and syncopated figures can turn a mundane chord sequence into an exciting piece of music. Notice how the rhythmic patterns never become predictable in "Fortune Accents." By bar five the pattern has changed and the chorus has a syncopation on the second half of beat three instead of four.

Example 7.2, "Fortune Accents"

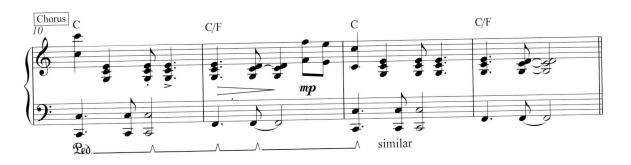

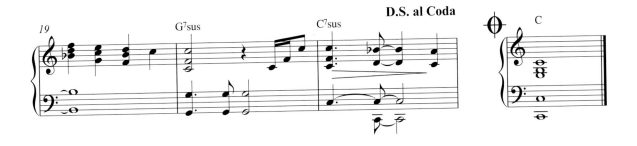

EIGHT-NOTE PATTERN

The chords are now broken up into an eighth-note pattern, which creates forward motion. This technique can be heard in the piano introduction to John Lennon's "Imagine." Bars five to eight have accents on the first, fourth, and seventh eighth-notes to tie in with the altered bass pattern. The left hand takes over the eighth-note pattern in the chorus with some passing notes added to the basic arpeggio. The key here is variation, particularly with a repetitive chord sequence. Having said that, a band like Coldplay often use repetitive piano parts whilst the other instruments create the variation.

There are an infinite number of ways to arrange this tune. Try playing around with the inversions of the chords. For example, in bar one you could play C and A above middle C on the first eighth-note, followed by E above middle C on the second eighth-note. Don't restrict yourself purely to chord tones; notice how the D minor chord in bar five has the G added.

Pro tip

Most ideas come from experimentation and improvisation. Don't get hung up on what's right and wrong; try things out and trust your ear to let you know what sounds good.

Example 7.3, "Broken Fortune"

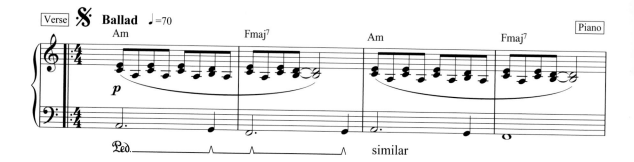

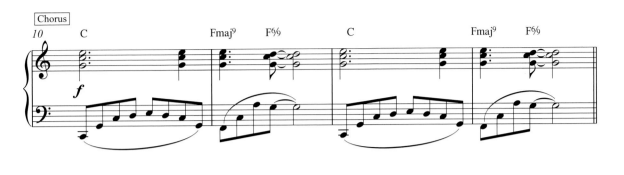

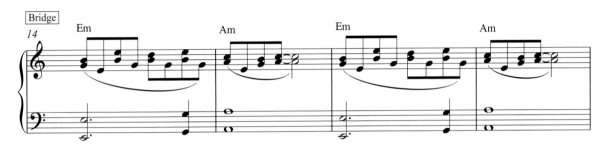

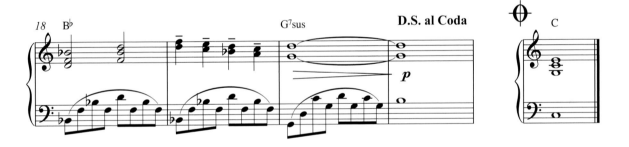

The last reworking of this tune uses arpeggios. If you look at bars one and two, the chords have been broken up and extra scale tones added (the F in bar one and the D in bar two).

By accenting these notes a clear melodic line can be heard to come out of the eighth-note pattern. The arpeggios give the song a lighter feel so the chorus has been pared down accordingly.

All of the various techniques we've looked at so could be combined together or used in various combinations within a single song.

Why not write your own tune now, drawing on the "Fortune" ideas for inspiration?

Pro tip

Arpeggios and scales are fundamental to all instruments but a vital part of any keyboard player's vocabulary. Try and put aside some time each day to work on these basics and gradually work your way through all the keys.

Example 7.4, "Fortune Arpeggios"

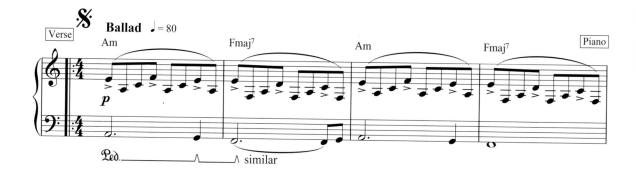

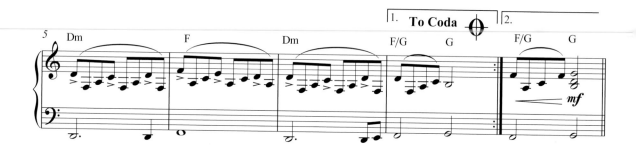

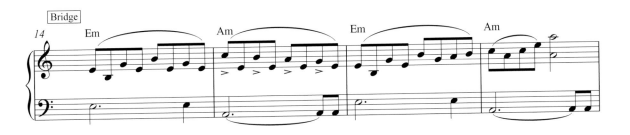

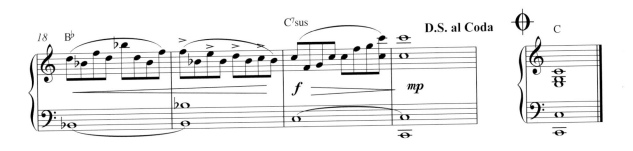

There's a reason why the piano is often referred to as part of the rhythm section. It really is a percussive instrument and can lend a lot of rhythmic power to a song. In salsa music, for instance, the piano is used to create repetitive rhythmic patterns called "montunos." And as you've seen earlier in this tutorial, it can be the driving force behind many styles, including rock'n'roll.

This next tune, "Heavy-Handed," is in pop-rock style and is the sort of part you would play within a band. It uses a strong chordal part in the right hand with a hard-hitting left-hand octave bass line; if you double up this bassline with the bass guitar it is a very powerful sound. The songs of Maroon 5 are a good example of using the piano in this way.

Play "Heavy-Handed" using a bright sampled piano sound on your keyboard. Keep your left hand very relaxed, and use the weight of your arm to get the octave accents. There is a new chord symbol in bars two and six. C#Ø7 stands for C-sharp half-diminished seventh or C-sharp minor seventh flat five. That's a diminished chord with a minor seventh rather than a diminished seventh.

Example 7.5, "Heavy-Handed"

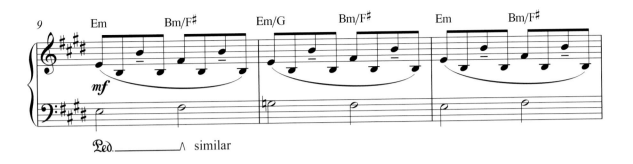

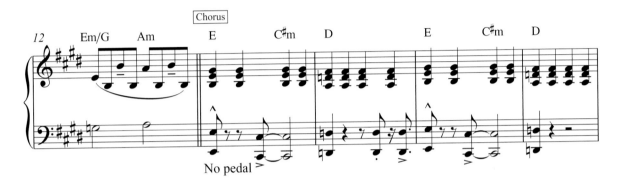

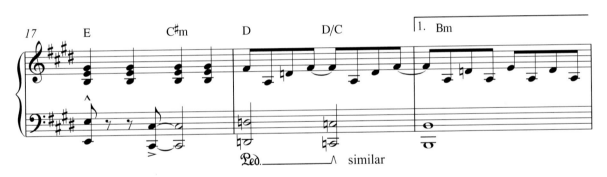

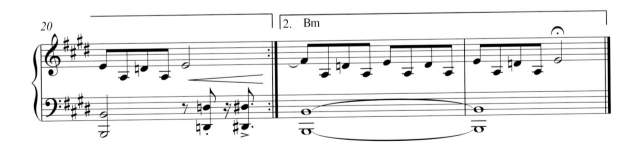

Here's another approach to the same song. "Light-Fingered" uses arpeggios and then, in the chorus, switches to the four-to-a-bar chord technique that we came across when we were looking at piano ballad style. These techniques work equally well in uptempo tunes. Use a mellow sampled-piano sound and the pedal throughout to create a sustained texture.

The accents in the right hand in bars one to seven outline a simple melodic line. Be sure to bring these notes out and give less weight to the other chord tones.

The left hand chords in the chorus should be played with a slight gap between each chord.

Pro tip

Octave melodies, as in the chorus here, sound great but can be hard to play. The trick is to keep a very relaxed wrist. If there's a large interval, use a curved movement with the arm rather than trying to stay parallel with the keyboard.

Example 7.6, "Light-Fingered"

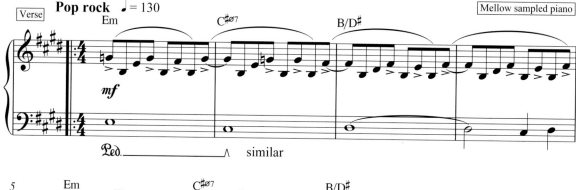

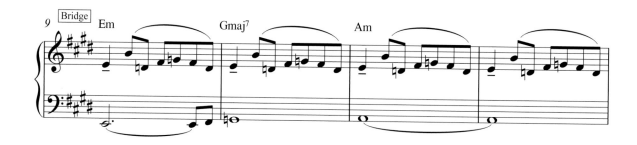

Keyboards play a very important role in mainstream indie music, particularly as many of the songwriters are pianists, including Chris Martin from Coldplay and Tim Rice-Oxley from Keane. What's interesting is that they are mixing up the old with the new, using modern synthesizers like the Clavia Nord Lead 3 and the Yamaha 90ES with older acoustic instruments like the Fender Rhodes and Hammond Organ.

Although not a new idea, the ability to combine sampled piano sounds with synth sounds opens up a whole new sonic world. Yamaha even brought out an acoustic piano that had MIDI fitted for the same purpose, but it was expensive and heavy to carry around.

The same effect can be achieved on a modern 88-note weighted keyboard. Weighted keyboards were originally invented to provide a portable alternative to the acoustic piano, one that could be amplified without all the technical difficulties that arise from miking up a real piano in a loud rock group. These keyboards have a weighted action similar to that of an acoustic piano. They quickly developed to incorporate synth sounds and effects, as well as enhanced programming capabilities so that splits and layers can be programmed and stored as a single patch.

"Eager" uses two keyboard sounds: a layered piano patch and an ambient pad. Meanwhile, a repeated note pattern on synth provides an underlying pulse.

Firstly find a piano sound and layer it with a pad. Layering is combining two or more sounds so that they can be played simultaneously and stored as a single patch. The beauty of this type of sound is that you have the percussive edge of the piano with the sustaining power of the pad coming in as you hold down the keys.

Secondly, you'll need to be able to set up a keyboard split (refer to Unit Six) so that you can play the ambient pad in your left hand. Pick a sound with a slow attack and some movement in it.

CD track 83 has the full version of "Eager" so you can hear the parts played with their relevant sounds.

Pro tip

If you are using a weighted keyboard you will be able to adjust the sensitivity of the action to suit your own playing style.

Example 7.7, "Eager"

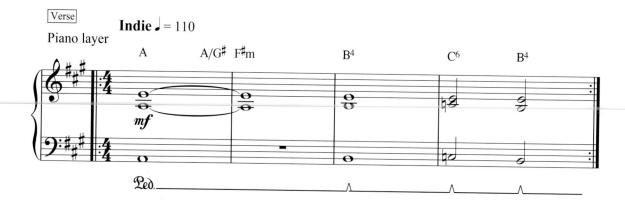

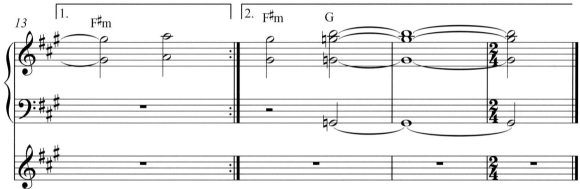

"Eager" Keyboard Set-Up

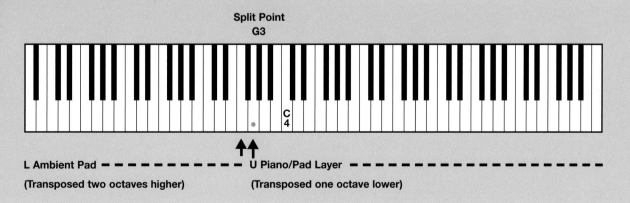

Split Point
G3

L Ambient Pad – – – – – – – – – **U Piano/Pad Layer** – – – – – – –

(Transposed two octaves higher)   **(Transposed one octave lower)**

As well as the more conventional sounds that you used in the last track, synthesizers can add texture and atmosphere. The underlying pulse of "Eager" is created by an arpeggiated synth. "Eager Two" has four additional synth sounds. These have been marked on the chord chart with an 'x' note to indicate where to play them, but the type of sound and the pitch is up to you. You may have to switch patches in order to access the four different sounds, but there is plenty of time to do this. All kinds of sounds can work, so you don't have to match them exactly to the sounds on the CD.

We now have seven separate parts. It would be impossible to play them all at once; however, the idea is to give you an example of the way in which different types of sounds can liven up a song. In a studio situation the keyboards would be multi-tracked and in a live setting some of the parts would be sequenced.

This is an opportunity for you to do your own thing. Using the chord sequence here, choose your own sounds and make up your own parts.

Example 7.8, "Eager Two"

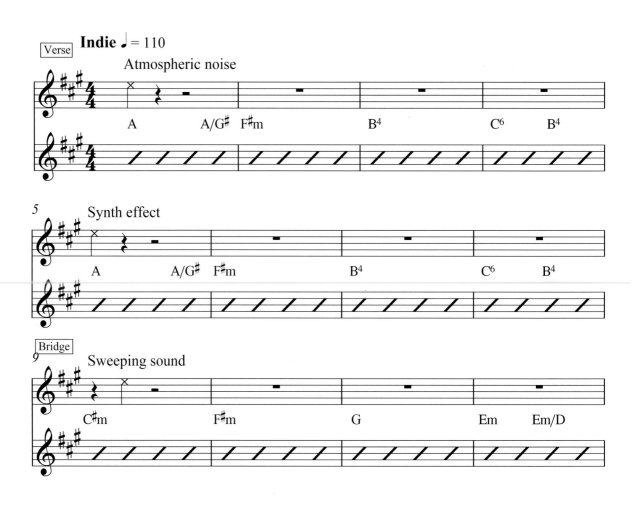

continued on next page

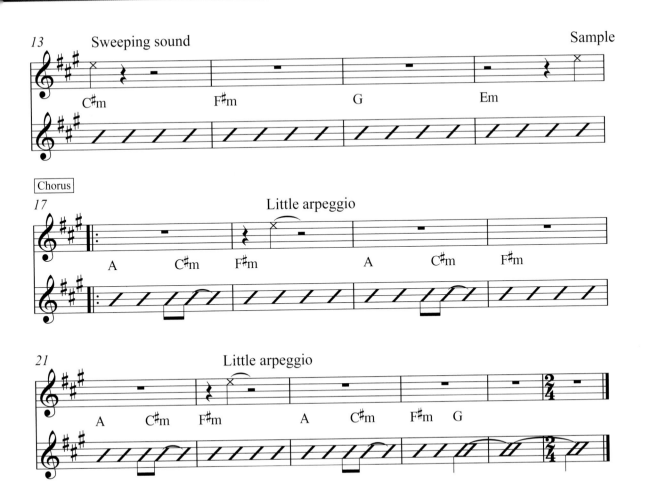

Sequencing and Dance Music

'Dance" is an all-encompassing term for a very broad genre of music. Well-known styles include disco, hardcore, garage, house, techno, trance, and electronica.

Its foundations were laid firmly in the late 70s with the advent of sequencing technology and the rise of a youth culture devoted to dancing.

The elements of the music remain the same today: a pumping rhythm track, layered with various synth parts generated by sequencing software, and topped off with a sprinkling of vocals.

We are going to look at the basics of sequencing, which you can apply to a keyboard workstation or a computer-based software sequencing program, like Steinberg's Cubase or Apple's Logic, and build up a basic dance number. Each sequencing program or keyboard workstation will have its own specifications so please consult the manual for more in-depth information.

Let's start by getting a few terms under our belt.

Sequencing

Sequencing is really a glorified word for multitracking. In the old days in recording studios, music was recorded on to separate tracks on magnetic tape, which could be layered on top of each other in the final mix.

Sequencing differs from audio multitracking in that each track can contain different data: for example, MIDI data, digital audio data, and control data. The old tape system had a finite number of tracks whereas modern sequencing software is limitless, depending on the speed of your computer and its storage capacity.

Quantization

Quantizing was originally developed to correct bad timing. When the quantize function is deployed, recorded MIDI information will be fixed to a pre-defined timing grid. The user specifies a "quantize number" to define the basic unit of time that MIDI notes will be fixed to. The result is an absolutely regular, metronomic performance.

But because real musicians do not play metronomically, software manufacturers quickly realized that they needed to develop more sophisticated quantizing templates that emulated real grooves.

Now here's where it gets mathematical. Each note can be seen as a subdivision of a bar, so in order to quantize correctly you will need to understand the chart below. A tick is the smallest unit of time a MIDI system uses: not all manufacturers use the same resolution.

Note name	Length of note	Quantize number	Ticks
Whole note	One bar	1	960
Half-note	Half a bar	2	480
Quarter-note	Quarter of a bar	4	240
Eighth-note	Eighth of a bar	8	120
16th-note	16th of a bar	16	60
32nd-note	32nd of a bar	32	30
64th-note	64th of a bar	64	15

Note Velocities

A MIDI note velocity is similar to the speed at which you strike a key on the piano; the resultant tone will vary according to that speed. By varying note velocities it is possible to instill some human feel into the music. The value can be set anywhere from 0–127.

General MIDI (GM)

General MIDI was developed just after MIDI came out. It sets a standard for a common set of sounds with specific program change numbers. If you use GM you can take your sequenced song and play it on another sequencer and it will play back using a similar set of sounds. This cuts down the time you would spend having to re-assign sounds to your song unnecessarily.

In this section we are going to build up the tracks needed to play "Dizzy," starting with drums.

The Drum Set

The sounds used in dance music are based on the traditional drum set. On top of that you will also find percussion sounds, like tambourine, cabasa, and handclap, and numerous beeps and squeaks. In "Dizzy" you need these sounds:

- Bass drum
- Snare drum
- Closed high hat
- Open high hat
- Clap
- Cymbals

Some drum patches replicate sounds taken from drum machines. Two of the most popular were Roland's TR 808 and 909. See if you have either of these; if not find a drum patch you like and assign it to a track.

If you're using a GM set of sounds the drums are on MIDI channel 10 and are given note numbers and assigned to keys on the keyboard following the GM standard (as explained on the following page).

You can either play the parts in real time using a metronome or input them in step time using the drum grid or matrix editor of your sequencing program. Quantizing locks them to the beat.

Most dance tunes are built out of four-bar or eight-bar patterns with some element of variation. We are going to start by individually programming the four-bar patterns and then building up a song from them.

Example 7.9, "Dizzy"

Start by programming the bass drum:

- Set the tempo to 130 beats per minute (bpm). Most dance tracks have tempos between 102 and 132 bpm, which is similar to the speed of a human heartbeat when exercising.
- Input the four-bar bass drum pattern, as shown in Example 7.9.
- Quantize bars one to three to a quantize factor of four and bar four to a quantize factor of eight. Quantizing locks the drum to the beat and removes any timing errors you may have made when playing the part.
- Adjust the bass drum velocities so that the first beat of each bar has a higher velocity, creating an accent.

Carry on in the same way with the rest of the drums and play around with the note velocities. Here are the quantize factors to be used for the other parts of the drum kit:

Instrument	Quantize factor
Bass drum	8
Snare	16
Closed hi-hat	16
Open hi-hat	8
Clap	4
Crash	4

General MIDI Standard Drum Set

NN	Note	Drum Sound	NN	Note	Drum Sound	NN	Note	Drum Sound
27	D# 0	High Q	48	C 2	High Tom 2	69	A 3	Cabasa
28	E 0	Slap	49	C# 2	Crash 1	70	A# 3	Maracas
29	F 0	Scratch Push	50	D 2	High Tom 1	71	B 3	Short Whistle
30	F# 0	Scratch Pull	51	D# 2	Ride 1	72	C 4	Long Whistle
31	G 0	Sticks	52	E 2	Chinese Cymbal	73	C# 4	Short Guiro
32	G# 0	Square Click	53	F 2	Ride Bell	74	D 4	Long Guiro
33	A 0	Metronome Click	54	F# 2	Tambourine	75	D# 4	Claves
34	A# 0	Metronome Bell	55	G 2	Splash	76	E 4	Hi Wood Block
35	B 0	Kick Drum 2	56	G# 2	Cowbell	77	F 4	Lo Wood Block
36	C 1	Kick Drum 1	57	A 2	Crash 2	78	F# 4	Mute Cuica
37	C# 1	Side Stick	58	A# 2	Vibra Slap	79	G 4	Open Cuica
38	D 1	Snare 1	59	B 2	Ride 2	80	G# 4	Mute Triangle
39	D# 1	Hand Clap	60	C 3	Hi Bongo	81	A 4	Open Triangle
40	E 1	Snare 2	61	C# 3	Lo Bongo	82	A# 4	Shaker
41	F 1	Low Tom 2	62	D 3	Mute Conga	83	B 4	Jingle Bell
42	F# 1	Closed Hi-Hat	63	D# 3	Hi Conga	84	C 5	Bell Tree
43	G 1	Low Tom 1	64	E 3	Lo Conga	85	C# 5	Castanets
44	G# 1	Pedal Hi-Hat	65	F 3	Hi Timbale	86	D 5	Mute Surdo
45	A 1	Mid Tom 2	66	F# 3	Lo Timbale	87	D# 5	Open Surdo
46	A# 1	Open Hi-Hat	67	G 3	Hi Agogo			
47	B 1	Mid Tom 1	68	G# 3	Lo Agogo			

Basslines

It was Donna Summer's 1977 hit " I Feel Love," produced by Giorgio Moroder, that set the benchmark for the robotic-sounding basslines that were to become intrinsic to dance music.

Its best to stick to a simple chord sequence. The bass should play off of the bass drum and give the music some drive and energy.

The bassline to "Dizzy" accentuates the first two bass-drum beats and has a syncopated rhythm around beats three and four. Program it like this:

- Chose a bass sound and assign it to a sequencer track.
- Input the four-bar synth bass pattern.
- Quantize to a quantize factor of 16.
- Accent beats one and two by giving them higher velocity levels.
- Adjust note lengths.

The way the bassline is written is intended to make reading easier. In fact the note lengths should be short to give a bouncy feel to the bassline, so set them all to the value of a 16th-note.

Synth Parts

When it comes to synth parts there are many possibilities. "Dizzy" has four contrasting parts. It's important to pick sounds that will blend but also be distinctive enough to stand out.

Part one is a pad, which creates a bed of sound. Part two is a sync part, which creates rhythm (rather like a guitar part). Part three is synth chords, which add rhythm and harmony. Part four is a lead line, which adds melodic interest. Program the synthesizer parts like this:

- Listen to the CD to get an idea of the sounds you need.
- Input the four keyboard parts, assigning each to a different track.
- Quantize according to the table below.
- Adjust note lengths and velocities.

Instrument	Quantize
Pad	4
Sync part	16
Synth chords	16
Lead line	16

STRUCTURE AND FORM

It's time to piece the jigsaw puzzle together. You now have 12 individual four-bar parts that can be pieced together in any order or combination.

The track on the CD has been put together in typical dance fashion with the bass drum starting and the rest of the parts being gradually phased in at four or eight-bar intervals, until we reach a breakdown section (left), where several parts are taken out and the pad introduced.

The final section introduces the sync part and brings in all the previous parts, some with slight variations.

Have a go at building up your own song. Use the copy, repeat, or loop functions of your sequencer and use the mute function to try out different combinations. Dance music is all about creating tension and releasing it. Your aim should be to build up, break down, and build up even higher again.

> **Pro tip**
> Always re-name any sequence that you alter, otherwise it can become very confusing.

Example 7.10, "Dizzy" Breakdown Section

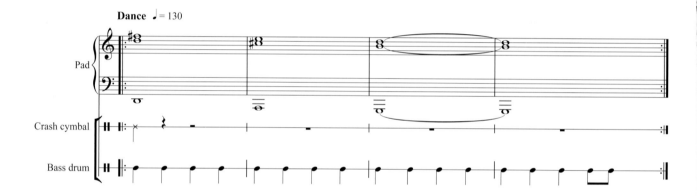

FILLS

Now that you've got the basic track in place let's add some fills.

Fills

It's common to signal a change in the music with a fill. This can be done on the snare drum or bass drum or a mixture of the two. Example 7.11 gives you some possibilities to try out. Program the individual four-bar patterns as before and insert them into the song where appropriate. Have a go at making up your own fills.

Variation

Most dance tracks, although repetitive, will introduce an element of variation from time to time and bring in new parts as the song progresses.

Some simple options can be to change the basic four-bar patterns by adding to or subtracting from them. Otherwise you can change the sound of a part, or change its octave or pitch by transposing it.

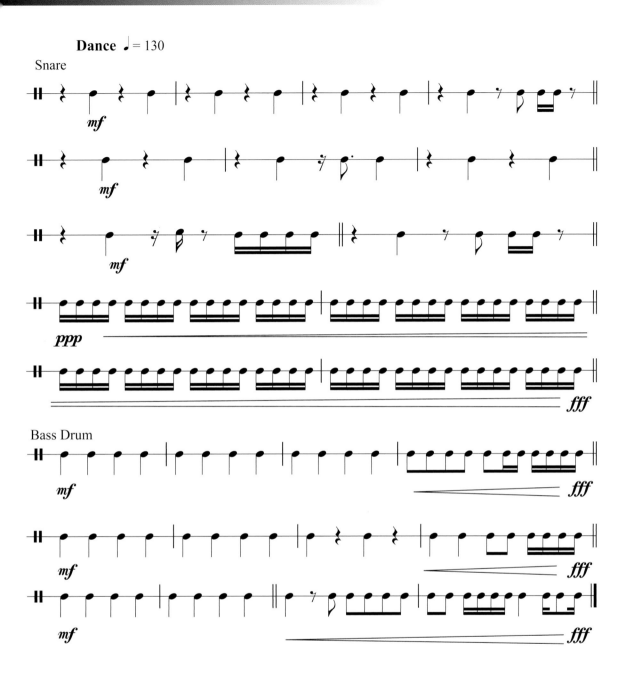

We've only seen the tip of the iceberg when it comes to sequencing and dance music. Hopefully, this will have given you an insight into what's involved and the desire to explore the music and the technology further.

GLOSSARY

Action The mechanism by which a piano makes a sound.

Additive synthesis System in which waveforms tuned to different harmonics are combined.

ADSR (Attack, Decay, Sustain, Release) Part of a synthesizer that controls the loudness of its sound over time.

Aftertouch A MIDI control signal that generates a message based on the pressure exerted on a key.

Amplifier Electronic circuit that increases the level of a signal.

Analog (UK: analogue) Relating to signals created by a continuously variable voltage; as opposed to digital.

Arpeggiator Device or setting for creating automatic arpeggios.

Arpeggio Playing the notes of a chord one at a time.

Attack Speed at which a sound reaches its maximum level.

Audio interface A device that routes audio into and out of a computer.

Barrelhouse Piano style of the early 20th century.

Bebop Type of jazz originating in the 40s and notable for its complex harmonies and rhythms.

Bit depth The number of bits used to represent a single sample in an audio file.

Channel (1) Path through which signal passes. (2) Path for MIDI data.

Check Mechanism that prevents a piano hammer from bouncing back and striking the string more than once.

Clock speed Speed at which a computer processes information.

Combo Amplifier and loudspeaker in the same box.

'Comping Accompanying a solo in jazz.

Compression Reducing the dynamic range of an audio signal.

Compressor Hardware or software system for compression.

Controller Device used to send MIDI messages, for instance a MIDI keyboard.

Control surface Mixer-like device that provides physical control of a software instrument.

Damping System that cuts off the sound of piano strings when a key is released.

DAW (Digital Audio Workstation) Hardware device or computer software that permits audio and MIDI recording, editing, and mixing.

Decay Gradual drop in level of a sound or signal.

Decibel (dB) Unit for measuring audio levels.

Digital Relating to signals that are created from a series of numbers (binary 1s and 0s); as opposed to analog.

DSP (Digital Signal Processor) A device used to process digital audio.

Duophonic Capable of playing two notes at once.

Effect (FX) Term for audio processing such as distortion, delay, reverberation, and so on.

Envelope generator Part of a synthesizer that controls the loudness of the sound over time.

Equalization (EQ) Tone control.

Escapement Part of piano action that allows the string to continue to vibrate after it has been struck.

Event Any MIDI occurrence or change, such as hitting or releasing a controller key.

Filter Electronic device or circuit that allows only certain frequencies to pass.

Firewire Interface for connecting peripherals to a computer.

FM (Frequency Modulation) Type of digital synthesis.

Gain Amount of increase of signal level. When dBs are used, increased gain is shown as +dB; reduction is –dB.

Gliss (Glissando) A glide from one pitch to another.

Harmonic An overtone created at the same time as the fundamental tone of an instrument.

Hub Device that allows you to expand the number of connections in your system.

Input A connection that allows signal or control information to enter a system.

Interface A device that routes signal to or from a computer, either a MIDI interface or an audio interface.

Jack (UK: socket) Mono or stereo connecting socket, usually quarter-inch.

Leslie Speaker system using revolving horns, often used with a Hammond organ.

LFO (Low-Frequency Oscillator) Synthesizer component that creates pulsating rhythms rather than audio tones.

Loop (1) v. To repeat. (2) n. Section of audio or MIDI that repeats.

Manual One keyboard on a multi-keyboard instrument, for instance an organ.

MIDI (Musical Instrument Digital Interface) Industry-standard system for transmitting and receiving notes in electronic instruments and computers.

MIDI interface Device for connecting MIDI instruments to a computer.

Mix (1) v. To combine multiple audio signals for output. (2) n. The combined audio recording that results.

Mixer Device for collecting, processing, and combining audio signals.

Modeling Technology that allows digital instruments to emulate analog synthesizers or acoustic instruments.

Modulation Audio effect that uses delay and pitch to alter a sound over time.

Modulation wheel Control on keyboard that adjusts modulation effects.

Multitrack A device capable of recording and playing back multiple tracks of audio.

Note In MIDI, a message that triggers a sound in a MIDI device.

Oscillator An electronic device or circuit that produces a fluctuating signal, often a sound.

Pad A synthesizer sound used for background harmony and atmosphere.

Pan Control that positions a sound in a stereo field.

Parameter Any aspect of a sound or device that can be controlled.

Patch (1) n. A combination of settings (for instance in a synthesizer) stored for later use. (2) v. To connect devices together.

Patchbay Device used to set up patches.

Patch cord Cable used to create patches.

PCM (Pulse Code Modulation) Standard method for encoding audio samples.

Pitch bend (1) MIDI message that alters the pitch of a note. (2) Keyboard control that alters the pitch of a note.

Plug-in Software that adds capabilities to a system. Includes effects processors and software instruments.

Polyphonic Of synthesizers, capable of playing several notes simultaneously.

RAM (Random Access Memory) Computer memory.

Reed Flat metal vibrating element used in some electric pianos.

Release The amount of time taken for a note to fade after a key is released.

Reverb (Reverberation) Ambience effect combining many short echoes.

Riff A repeated melodic or rhythmic figure.

Root The note in a chord or scale that gives it its name.

Sample (1) The smallest unit in a digital audio recording. (2) An audio recording that can be triggered by a sampler.

S & S (Sample and Synthesis) Digital synthesizer technique that combines samples with generated sounds.

Sampler A device that can record and play back audio samples at different pitches.

Semitone A half-step between notes; the smallest interval in Western music.

Sequencer A device or software program that stores and plays back MIDI information.

Signal processor A device that alters a signal, particularly for audio effects.

Soft synth A synthesizer that exists only as software.

Software instrument A software emulation of a physical instrument.

Split To set up a synthesizer keyboard so that different physical regions play different sounds.

Standard A tune or song of established popularity.

Star network System for connecting several MIDI devices to a central hub.

Stop Tone control on organ and some early pianos.

Stride Semi-improvised piano style of the early 20th century.

Sustain Length of time a note is held for.

Synchronize To lock two devices together so they play back together.

Syncopation Displacement of the normal beat.

Synthesizer Electronic instrument used for sound creation, using analog or digital techniques.

Tempo Speed of a musical passage.

Thru MIDI connection that passes information through one device to another.

Timbre Tone quality of a sound.

Time code Synchronization information.

Tine Vibrating element in a Fender Rhodes piano.

Tonewheel System of generating sounds used in the Hammond organ.

Track A channel of audio or MIDI information.

Transpose To change pitch or key of a musical passage or audio track.

Tremolo Rhythmic fluctuation of volume.

Unbalanced Cables and connectors using a single signal wire and a surrounding shield.

USB (Universal Serial Bus) Interface for connecting peripherals to a computer.

VCA (Voltage Controlled Amplifier) Envelope generator which controls the loudness of a sound over time.

VCF (Voltage Controlled Filter) A filter whose parameters are controlled by altering applied voltages.

VCO (Voltage Controlled Oscillator) An oscillator whose frequency is controlled by an applied voltage.

Velocity A MIDI parameter that measures the force with which a key is struck.

Vibrato Rhythmic fluctuation of pitch.

Virtual instrument A synthesizer existing only as software.

Voice Each of the sounds capable of being produced simultaneously by an electronic instrument.

Voltage control A system for controlling another circuit (for instance, an oscillator or an envelope generator) by altering a voltage.

Waveform A curve showing the shape of a wave at any given time.

XLR Three-pin audio connector.

ON THE CD

MUSIC CREDITS

"Major Tune," "Minor Tune," "Broken Triads," "Minor Triumph," "Quite Contrary," "Slow Sevenths," "Organ Donor," "Go with the Flow," "Curly Wurly," "Changing Times," "Snakepit Life," "Wonderful Harmony," "Gospel Celebration," "Peaches and Cream," "Funky Clav," "Choked Up," "Top Skanking," "Know Your Onions," "A La Mode," "Fifth Gear," "G Whizz," "Grand Designs," "Who Needs Friends?," "Mid Atlantic," "Brothers in Crime," "Rocks On," "Not Over Yet," "Heroic Times," "St Vitus," "Heavy Traffic," "Round the Houses," "Favorite Thing," "Angela's Added Ninths," "The Long Stretch," "No Smokin'," "Logical Dan," "Digest the Answer," "Nice Work if You Can," "Nutmeg City," "Run Don't Walk," "Dear Virginia," "Terry O'Meher," "Boogie Along," "Chrysalis," "Chrysalis Two," "Penta," "Market A.M.," "Market P.M.," "Joe's Friends," "Doctor Floyd," "Showtime," "Showtime Solo," "Hand Jive," "Play, Don't Feel," "Strange Dreams," "Quarter Past Five"
© 2008 Steve Lodder.

"Lucky Number 12," "Swing Thing," "Riffin'," "Barreling Along," "JM's Boogie," "Slip Slide," "Domino's Dance," "Riffin' Two," "Lonesome Blues," "Lonesome Blues Two," "Pretty Poly," "Small Town Girl," "The Apartment," "Disco Strings," "Disco Strings Two," "Disco Brass," "Disco Brass Two," "Popsicle," "Popsicle Split," "Fortune Smiles," "Fortune Accents," "Broken Fortune," "Fortune Arpeggios," "Heavy-Handed," "Light-Fingered," "Eager," "Eager Two," "Dizzy"
© 2008 Janette Mason.